P9-CFK-498

3 9153 00939335 8

THE MODERN NATIONS IN HISTORICAL PERSPECTIVE

ROBIN W. WINKS, *General Editor*

The volumes in this series deal with individual nations or groups of closely related nations throughout the world, summarizing the chief historical trends and influences that have contributed to each nation's present-day character, problems, and behavior. Recent data are incorporated with established historical background to achieve a fresh synthesis and original interpretation.

FREDERICK G. HEYMANN, the author of this volume, received his doctorate in political science from the Johann Wolfgang von Goethe University in Frankfurt. Professor of History at the University of Alberta, Calgary, he was a member of the Institute for Advanced Study, Princeton, in 1956-58, and 1966; among his other publications are *John Žižka and the Hussite Revolution*; *George of Bohemia, King of Heretics*; and numerous articles to scholarly journals.

ALSO IN THE EUROPEAN SUBSERIES

The Balkans *by Charles and Barbara Jelavich*, S-611
Italy *by Massimo Salvadori*, S-612
Scandinavia *by John H. Wuorinen*, S-614
France *by John C. Cairns*, S-617

Baltic Sea
POMERANIA
POLAND
U.S.S.R.
EAST GERMANY
WEST GERMANY
CZECHOSLOVAKIA
BOHEMIA
MORAVIA
SLOVAKIA
SILESIA
AUSTRIA
HUNGARY
RUMANIA
0
40
80
120
MILES
14°
18°
22°
24°
26°
54°
52°
50°
48°
Hamburg
Szczecin
(Stettin)
Gdynia
Gdańsk
Kaliningrad
Minsk
Bydgoszcz
Toruń
Mława
Łomża
Białystok
Inowrocław
Włocławec
Płock
Gniezno
Poznań
Bérlin
Warszawa
Kalisz
Łodz
Leipzig
Legnica
Wrocław
(Breslau)
Brzeg
Swidnica
Radom
Lublin
Kielce
Częstochowa
Bytom
Chorzów
Katowice
Gliwice
Cracow
Przemyśl
Nowy Sącz
Děčin
Jablonec
Most
Cheb
Praha
Pardubice
Plzeň
Písek
České
Budějovice
Jihlava
Brno
Znojmo
Opava
Ostrava
Cieszyn
Přerov
Žilina
Trenčin
Prešov
Košice
Zvolen
Nitra
Bratislava
Linz
Vienna
Budapest
Elbe
Odra
Vistula
Bug
Vltava
Morava
Danube
Tisza

POLAND & CZECHOSLOVAKIA

FREDERICK G. HEYMANN

A SPECTRUM BOOK

Prentice-Hall, Inc.

Englewood Cliffs, New Jersey

To Frank, Ruth, and Lou—
in common remembrance
and gratitude

 Library of Congress Catalog Card Number 66-22803. Printed in the United States of America—C. P 68494, C 68495

Current printing (last number):
10 9 8 7 6 5 4 3 2

Preface

This book deals with the history of the peoples of Poland and Czechoslovakia. It would be a mistake to conclude, however, that these two modern states and the nations from which they developed have anything like an essentially common history, or that they maintained, throughout the ages, an especially close relationship with one another. There are, it is true, important similarities. They are ethnically mainly West Slavs and speak closely related languages. All of them, Poles, Czechs, and Slovaks, were from early times under the strong impact of their great western neighbors, the Germans, an impact which, as a culturally fertilizing influence and as a lively challenge to their own cultural productivity, was often highly valuable, but which, in purely political terms, was more frequently a danger than a blessing, a deadly danger especially in the recent past. Yet in spite of this the West Slav nations failed to cooperate most of the time and instead were quite often at loggerheads (not unlike other nations closely related to each other, such as the Danes and the Swedes). The interrelationship between West Slav peoples is, thus, in itself an important but by no means the all-important topic of the story of each of them, and in writing a sketch of their history in one piece I had to be careful neither to neglect nor to overemphasize the part of this history that deals with their mutual relationship. Yet I thought it best to write this historical sketch essentially as one, i.e., to combine the development of both countries in each chapter, as this story unfolds, essentially on a chronological basis. I hope that the attempt to treat what are essentially two and, to some extent, even three national histories as if they were one will not make it more difficult for the reader to gain that first acquaintance with their development which is, I believe, the main purpose of this series. I do, indeed, believe such method of proceeding on parallel tracks may even help in the basic understanding of their history because it almost forces on author and readers a measure of that comparative approach to historiography which has, in recent times, become increasingly acknowledged as of considerable heuristical as well as didactical value.

This little book may well differ from others in this series by giving relatively more space to the earlier history of the West Slav nations, more not only in comparison with the younger nations (e.g., of the New World), but of other peoples who can also look back upon a thousand years or more of national development. The main reason for this emphasis on earlier historical roots lies in the fact that the West Slav nations are intensely history-conscious, probably more so than most other modern nations, especially in their constant relating to events and developments that go back over many centuries. This, again, is partly due to the fact that in the early seventeenth-century Bohemia, and a century and a half later Poland, became victims of foreign attacks which for a while seemed to eliminate them as free and active members of the European comity of nations, while the Slovaks even had to go back to the earlier Middle Ages to find a time in which they had not been a rather inconspicuous member of the group of nations joined under the Crown of St. Stephen. To find and reconfirm their full and rich national heritage and identity, therefore, modern Poles, Czechs, and Slovaks had perforce to go back to much earlier times. There they could, indeed, find a marvelous wealth of national achievement which would also give higher meaning to their appearance as modern nations. Their own historical perspective goes back to the Middle Ages and the times of the Reformation and the Renaissance. Without presenting, however sketchily, such phases as the ages of Charles IV and Casimir the Great or, following these, the Hussite Revolution and Reformation in Bohemia or the development of state and society in the Renaissance Poland of the Jagellons, it would not be possible even to approach the ideas that dominate the historical consciousness and with it the actions and reactions of the West Slav nations to this day.

Clearly the attempt to sketch and interpret in a slim volume some of the dominant but complex issues which arose in the history of these nations demands an unusually large measure of selection and condensation. It is a question not only of what to include but more often of what to omit. I have found this choice not always an easy task, and I am grateful to Professors Peter Brock of Columbia University and Stanley Pech of the University of British Columbia for the advice they have given me after reading the draft of this volume.

F.G.H.

Contents

ONE

"Contemporary History": Two Decades Since Yalta

The history of Poland and Czechoslovakia is, and has been for many centuries, of great importance to the history of mankind. World War II—an event whose outcome still shapes the lives of people all over the world—broke out over the German conquest of Czechoslovakia (indirectly) and Poland (directly). Because Hitler was determined to embark on a great war of conquest, it is fair to say that World War II would have occurred in any case after the European powers had permitted the reestablishment of a gigantic German war machine. Yet the specific role of the two West Slav states was far more than merely incidental and was of greater significance than was the role of Serbia in World War I. The "living-space" that Adolf Hitler was determined to conquer for Germany could be gained only in the East, and he thought and planned in terms of the vast lands of Russia and the Ukraine. Thus Czechoslovakia and Poland, Germany's immediate neighbors, both allied to Germany's greatest western neighbor, France, presented the first barrier to the program of a continent-wide expansion. Hitler's final occupation of mutilated Czechoslovakia made it clear even to appeasement-minded people that the compromise of Munich could not and did not work as a peaceful settlement and that the Western powers, if they wanted to survive, would be forced to fight the next stage of Nazi aggression. In substance the great holocaust had become unavoidable in the fall of 1938 (perhaps more so than did World War I in the weeks immediately following the murder of Archduke Francis Ferdinand), and even more so in March 1939, although the open outbreak did not occur until Poland was invaded in early September, first by German troops and later, on the basis of the Nazi-Soviet alliance concluded in August, by Soviet forces.

If the crucial role of the two West Slav countries, especially in terms of military and political geography, had not been fully understood in the West before and during World War II, it should have become quite obvious in the light of the next great conflict—the "Cold War" between the states belonging to the Atlantic alliance (usually thought of as the NATO powers) and the countries of the Soviet orbit. Here the sequence was reversed. If, in 1938-39, Czechoslovakia was the first victim and Poland the second, in the postwar years it was largely the fate of Poland that destroyed the seemingly close warborn friendship between the English-speaking powers and Stalin's Russia. Following the change that took place in Czechoslovakia in 1948 the struggle took on a new dimension. If Stalin and his disciples had, even during the war, taken it for granted that the Western powers were in truth not friends but clandestine enemies, the West, too, now became convinced that they had to look upon Stalin and his realm as adversaries.

The difficulties between the West and the Soviet Union over Poland had their origins in events that took place during the war. At its beginning the eastern part of the Polish Republic, especially those territories inhabited by large numbers of Ukrainians and Byelorussians, had, in agreement with Germany, been occupied by Soviet forces, but upon the German invasion of the Soviet Union in June 1941 the whole of Poland was occupied by the Nazis, who subjected the country to fearful ravages. The Polish government in exile, headed by General Sikorski, concluded peace and soon afterward formed a treaty of alliance with the Soviet government. There was also a close cooperation between the Polish government in exile and its Czechoslovak counterpart, headed by President Eduard Beneš, which went so far as to envisage a federal union between them. But before long Polish-Soviet relations suffered setbacks—the most striking in April 1943, when the Germans announced that they had found mass-graves of thousands of Polish officers in the Forest of Katyn, near Smolensk. The Polish government, which even earlier had been disturbed by the disappearance of large numbers of Polish officers who had been Russian prisoners of war, demanded an investigation by the International Red Cross, a request which Moscow answered by breaking off relations with the Polish government. Today it seems likely that the dead of Katyn were victims of one of Stalin's or Beria's crimes, but at the time few in the allied camp were ready to believe this and were understandably inclined to assume one more case of Nazi genocide. Thus the Polish government, in this sudden isolation, found little support from the two great Western powers, who were unable to act decisively as long as the Western Front had not been established and a Soviet-German separate peace seemed possible. There was sympathy in the West for the Soviet demand—strongly resented by the Polish government—that the Russian-Polish border be shifted westward to the so-called Curzon Line, so as to agree more closely with ethnic frontiers. While Western statesmen indulged in the illusion that a Poland without large Ukrainian and Byelorussian minorities would be less apt to be subject to Soviet interference, Stalin had already prepared everything for the creation of a Polish state which would in fact, if not in name, be ruled from Moscow just as the greater central region of partitioned Poland had been ruled by the tsars from St. Petersburg all through the nineteenth century. The first step in this direction was taken in Lublin, one of the first Polish cities gained by the Russian offensive, when a Committee of Poles acceptable to Stalin was officially recognized by the Soviet Union as the provisional government of Poland. The next decisive step followed during the Big Three meeting at Yalta in February 1945. The two Western powers attempted to save for Poland at least the city of Lwów (then an essentially Polish place, though surrounded by a mostly Ukrainian countryside) and the oil fields of Galicia, but gave in when Stalin insisted on the original Curzon Line with a minor correction in favor of the Soviet Union. Poland, so the understanding was, would be compensated by corresponding gains in the west which would give her the Oder and Western Neisse rivers as border lines from the Baltic Sea to Czechoslovakia. Though this border was not officially fixed until the Conference of Potsdam soon after the end of the war—and even then was declared to be provisional and subject to the decision of a final peace conference—the fact remained that the Western allies in principle approved the idea of pushing Poland some 120 to 150 miles westward. As a result Germany was to lose, of the territory she had had from 1919 to 1937, the provinces of East Prussia (the northern half was annexed by the USSR, the south went to Poland) and Silesia (with its capital of Breslau), most of Pomerania (with the capital and port city of Stettin), and a large part of the province of Brandenburg. In view of the terrible sufferings that the Polish people had had to undergo throughout the war years at the hands of the German occupation forces, it is understandable enough that the Allied statesmen, including the leaders of America and Britain, did not at this stage feel much compassion for the German population in those territories who, if they had not fled westward before the Russian advance, suffered much hardship by being evacuated from those eastern provinces to German territories farther west. What the allied statesmen, whether British or American, did not seem to realize was that the great westward shift of Poland on the map was likely to make the new Poland, on the basis of its political geography, thoroughly dependent on the protection of its huge eastern neighbor, the Soviet Union.

Even with this high degree of Polish dependence, Stalin was by no means willing to give the Polish people any chance for internal development on the basis of democratic self-determination. At Yalta he had conceded, after long and sometimes bitter haggling, especially with Churchill, that the Lublin Committee, in order to receive recognition from the West as the true government of Poland, "should be recognized on a democratic basis with the inclusion of democratic leaders from Poland itself and from Poles abroad." Yet it was only with the greatest difficulty that American diplomacy obtained the inclusion, in this Russian-sponsored government, of a very few "independent democratic leaders," most important among them the leader of the Peasant party and former head of the London Polish government, Stanisław Mikolajczyk. His presence in the new Polish government as Vice-Premier and Minister of Agriculture made it easier for foreign governments, especially those of the West, to transfer recognition from the London "government in exile" to the Moscow-sponsored one; and it also seemed to guarantee that Poland would not go the way of the Soviet Union in destroying the peasant ownership of land in favor of general collectivization of agriculture. Poland has, indeed, so far, avoided going to such extremes, yet this was not Mikolajczyk's work. In 1947, at the first elections held (they had already been promised at Yalta), Mikolajczyk protested against harsh measures of rigging and intimidation which left his party—earlier the largest in Poland—with only 10 per cent of the officially announced votes and only about 6 per cent representation in the *Sejm* (Diet).

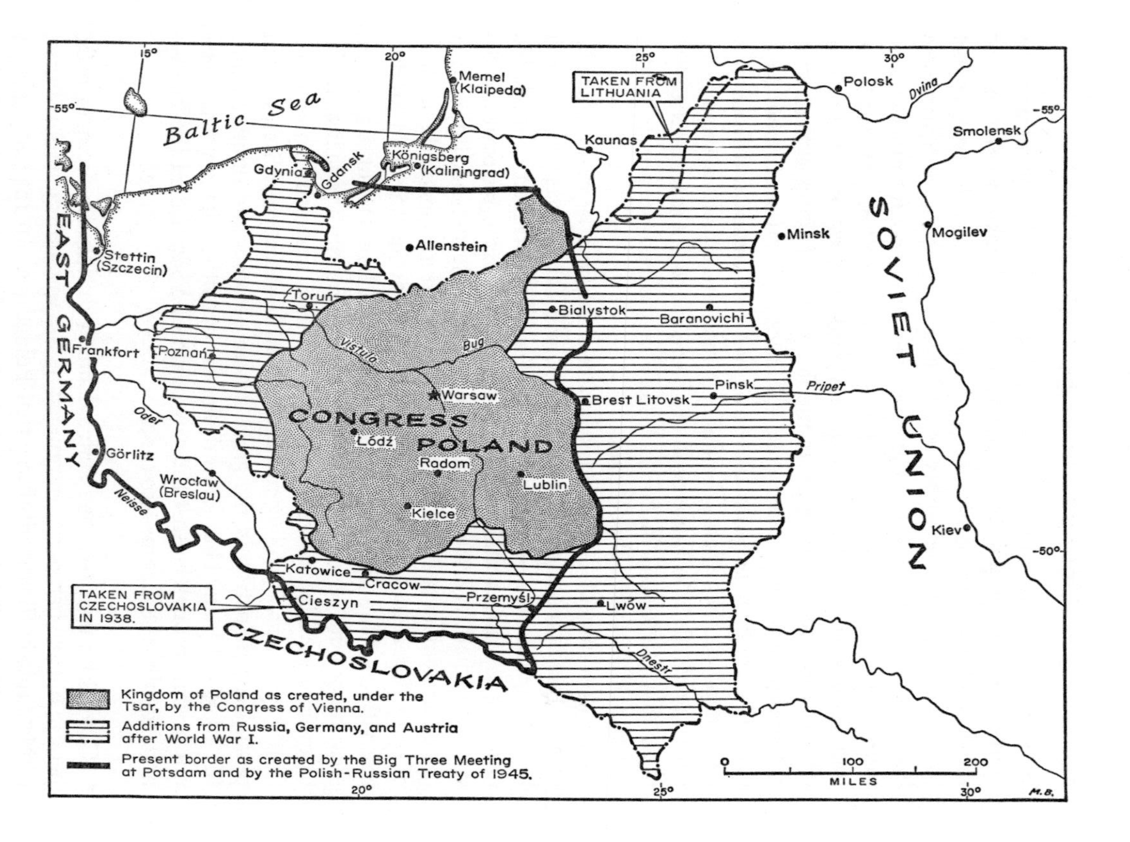
Baltic Sea
Memel (Klaipeda)
Königsberg (Kaliningrad)
Gdynia
Gdansk
Stettin (Szczecin)
Allenstein
Kaunas
TAKEN FROM LITHUANIA
Polosk
Dvina
Smolensk
Mogilev
Minsk
SOVIET UNION
Kiev
Toruń
Vistula
Bug
Bialystok
Baranovichi
Frankfort
Poznań
Warsaw
Pinsk
Pripet
Brest Litovsk
CONGRESS POLAND
Łódź
Radom
Lublin
Kielce
Oder
Görlitz
Wrocław (Breslau)
Neisse
EAST GERMANY
Katowice
Cracow
Cieszyn
Przemyśl
Lwów
Dnestr
TAKEN FROM CZECHOSLOVAKIA IN 1938.
CZECHOSLOVAKIA
Kingdom of Poland as created, under the Tsar, by the Congress of Vienna.
Additions from Russia, Germany, and Austria after World War I.
Present border as created by the Big Three Meeting at Potsdam and by the Polish-Russian Treaty of 1945.
0
100
200
MILES
15°
20°
25°
30°
55°
50°
M.B.

As a result of this conflict he had to leave the government and the country. If Polish policy, nevertheless, later shook off some of the most painful fetters of Stalinist oppression this was due to the fact that, among the Communists as well as the left-wing Socialists who had formed the main part of the Moscow-sponsored government, there were men and, indeed, groups of men who were Poles first and Communists or left-wing Socialists second, and who resented the way in which, under Stalin and even in the first phase of the post-Stalin era, the country was actually run (and exploited) by emissaries from Moscow. The conflicts between these anti-Stalinist groups and the Stalinists among the Poles, and the difficult movements and maneuverings which resulted from those conflicts form, indeed, a large part of the more dynamic events in Polish history in the two decades following the end of the German occupation.

Any government of Poland, whether right, left, or center, would, during the immediate postwar years, have found itself faced by a truly herculean task—the rebuilding of a terribly ruined country. No other European capital had been so utterly and systematically destroyed as had Warsaw. Even in the potentially rich territories that the Poles took over from Germany they found an incredible amount of ruins that it took a long time to turn into living cities and productive villages. How bad the situation was, and how urgent a generous measure of outside help appeared, can be seen from the fact that this Communist-guided government, without first asking for permission from Moscow, was willing to negotiate with the United States about possible participation in the great system of economic support called the Marshall Plan. This act of deviation from the Moscow line could not be put through against the way in which Stalin called the Poles—and, equally, the Czechs—to order.

Czechoslovakia, too, had suffered much during the German occupation, but she had not been ravaged by the war and the monstrosities of Nazi rule in the dreadful way that Poland had. In 1945 the country seemed to be able to revive a large part of her political traditions, which the Nazi occupation had temporarily destroyed. Dr. Beneš, the second president of Czechoslovakia, could return from his London exile via Moscow and could hope to reestablish a democracy, essentially libertarian in its political structure, though leaning toward socialism in the economic field. That this hope was thwarted, that instead a violent change in February 1948 turned Czechoslovakia, too, into a Stalinist satellite, was the outcome of internal struggles intimately connected with the Cold War.

Dr. Beneš personally had cherished the illusion that Stalin was in earnest when he assured him that the Soviet Union would not interfere in Czechoslovakia's national policy. The first rude awakening from this dream came in July 1947 when Czechoslovakia, whose prime minister was Klement Gottwald, head of the Communist party, but which like Poland was in urgent need of economic help, decided to accept the invitation to take part in the Paris negotiations on the Marshall Plan. Stalin, in a manner reminiscent of the way in which Hitler had treated smaller government heads, summoned the Czech Prime Minister—he had gone to Moscow for other reasons—and forced him and his colleagues by unmistakable threats to reverse their decision. The Prague government, it became clear, had no freedom of action. From now on Gottwald, to justify himself before Stalin as a true Communist, had to strengthen and speed up the program of eliminating all non-Communist or anti-Communist elements in the country from positions of any real influence.

The plan to transform Czechoslovakia from a multiparty state with a government based on free elections into a close copy of the Soviet Union had existed for a considerable time. It had been Beneš' policy to try to convince Stalin that his country, even if given complete freedom for its internal development, would be and would remain a close friend of the Soviet Union. Stalin had pretended to reciprocate this attitude, but his deep suspicion of all groups, countries, or individuals not completely under his control made him look upon a friendly but truly independent Czechoslovakia as untrustworthy. It is probable that Czechoslovakia, as a fully industrialized country with the capacity for producing the most highly developed machines for war and peace, was considered of greater importance to the Soviet bloc in its steadily growing antagonism to the West than any other territory that was at that time part of the Soviet sphere of influence. As long as the general trend in Czechoslovakia's political development seemed to run in favor of a more or less peaceful conquest of the governmental machinery by the Communist party and its close political friends among the Socialists there seemed to be no compelling reason to speed up this process. But in the winter 1947-48 it became, for the first time, doubtful whether this trend would persist. The growth of the Communist party had been rather spectacular up to this time, when it had reached one and one-third million members, and in the election to the Constituent Assembly in May 1946 they had received 38 per cent of the vote and 114 out of 300 seats. In the elections to a regular parliament slated for 1948—two years later—they claimed that they would at least gain 51 per cent of the vote, but the party's own polls indicated that the far more likely outcome would be a loss of votes which would, in all likelihood, have deprived the party of the traditional right to claim, as the largest single bloc, the prime-ministership. The whole relationship between the parties forming the coalition had, in the second half of 1947, steadily deteriorated, especially because the non-Communist parties (all of them center or left of center since none of the conservative parties had been admitted in 1945) felt deeply aggrieved about the increasing amount of purges of non-Communist elements of the police by its boss, the Communist minister of the interior. The situation worsened when Zdeněk Fierlinger, Czechoslovak ambassador to Moscow during the war and leader of the left wing of the Socialists, lost the position of chairman of the Socialist Party. The Communists now seemed isolated. Finally, in February 1948, the majority of the ministers of the non-Communist parties resigned, hoping that this would enable President Beneš to dissolve Parliament and have elections at an earlier date. This was clearly a tactical mistake, as it enabled the Communists to demand that the president accept the resignations. On this basis Gottwald would form a cabinet consisting entirely of Communists and a few left-wing Socialists. But even without this mistake the crisis would almost certainly have arisen, since the party, already impatient in the face of a prolonged coalition policy, at a time when all the rest of East Central Europe had been taken over by Communist governments, was certainly not willing to suffer what would have been the democratic consequences of an electoral defeat and give up some of its strongest positions in the administration of the republic. In any case, the long prepared organization of Communist-led action committees in all major factories and offices put an almost irresistible pressure on President Beneš, whose physical and nervous strength had largely been sapped by two recent brain hemorrhages. The sudden arrival of Stalin's East-European "trouble shooter," Valerian Zorin, made it clear that the Soviet Union was not willing to let things take any course not agreeable to Stalin, while it was equally clear that the Western powers were not ready to take any effective counteraction. A considerable number of the officers of the army in which the "Western sympathizers" had largely been isolated or removed by the Minister of War, the Moscow-trained General Svoboda, could probably be expected to back the prime minister, though until recently the president had doubted this. The vacillating attitude of the chairman of the Socialists, Laušman, seemed to indicate that there was no longer a reliable parliamentary majority standing up against the Communist action, and Beneš did not even retain the chance to appeal to the nation or the world by radio. On February 25, having resisted several days, he gave in and appointed the cabinet that Gottwald presented to him. This was the end of what the Communists called "bourgeois democracy." Many of its active representatives either fled the country or soon found themselves behind prison walls. Czechoslovakia's foreign minister, Jan Masaryk, the popular son of the founder of the republic whom the new regime wanted to keep in office for reasons of prestige at least for a while, died, probably by suicide. Dr. Beneš resigned from his office a few months later, on June 7. (He died soon afterward.) Elections were held even before the President's abdication, but in a way that offered the voter no alternatives, no free choice between candidates with differing points of view. This system was made still more rigid in the following elections—the next one being held in 1954.

The new regime, in its formal structure, retained some features that distinguished it from the Soviet system. Thus the office of President was retained—Gottwald now took over this position, and the second most important man in the Communist hierarchy, Antonín Zápotocký, like Gottwald a man of working-class origin, became prime minister. Since then this scheme, which gave a strong position to the head of the state, has been maintained. Zápotocký became president upon Gottwald's death in 1953, while Antonín Novotný became prime minister. Novotný followed Zápotocký in the presidency in 1957 and the Slovak Viliam Široký became prime minister. He stayed in office until the slow and almost mute struggle against Stalinism finally removed him in 1963 in favor of another Slovak, Josef Lenárt.

The new regime's first combative action had gone against the non-Communists, with the exception of the left-wing Socialists and a small number of other politicians whose unquestioning cooperation was meant to express the broad support given to the government by the nation as a whole. The peasantry, who had repeatedly been assured by the party that no collectivization based on the Soviet model was even contemplated, soon found themselves under severe pressure to join the collective farms, pressure so harsh as to equal in many ways Stalin's dreadful war against the Kulaks. In one decade, from 1949 to 1959, collectivized farms, or what was called the "socialist sector" of Czechoslovak agriculture, rose from 10.9 per cent of all agricultural land to 84.4 per cent. As a result of this Russian-type policy Czechoslovak agriculture, once quite healthy and progressive and able to feed the people of the Republic (who numbered in excess of a million more in the thirties than in the fifties) with little need for additional imports, now became, as Soviet agriculture long had been, one of the most backward and least productive parts of the economy and a permanent problem for the government. In the industrial field, socialization, already far advanced in the period from 1945 to 1948, was accelerated to the maximum during the next decade, leaving hardly a trace of free enterprise anywhere. But in industry, at least, vast engineering experience and previously high standards made possible a considerable increase in total production and a remarkable development of industrialization in Slovakia, which had long been less developed than the western provinces. Yet there were increasing complaints about the poor quality of industrial goods—those used on the domestic market as well as those intended for export (overwhelmingly to the Soviet Union and other Eastern European countries).

On the whole, the late 1940s and early '50s were surely one of the least happy periods of the country. Having so far stood half outside the actual dominion of Stalinist Russia, the leaders of the party now felt they had to prove their full Stalinist orthodoxy by all means available. At this time, important developments in Czechoslovakia can be traced back to Stalin's personal influence. This is especially striking in the case of the Czechoslovak reaction to the sudden rift between Stalin and Marshal Tito of Jugoslavia. Here the Stalinist attitude survived its author by several years. The propaganda war against Tito was conducted in Prague with a fervor surpassing that in most of the other eastern European countries. And it is at least partly in connection with this historic struggle that Prague, in 1950-51, saw one of the most horrifying Stalinist purge trials. Its two most prominent victims were Vlado Clementis, Jan Masaryk's successor as foreign minister, and Rudolf Slánský, a far more powerful man as secretary-general of the Communist party. In Clementis' case the accusation of Titoism, a sin which was largely equated with the heresies of "bourgeois nationalism" and "revisionism," was to some extent understandable. Clementis, after all, had been one of the "westerners" among the Communist leaders, had spent the years of the Nazi occupation first in Paris and then in London, and had, above all, dared openly to criticize Stalin's pact of friendship and near-alliance with Hitler. Stalin never forgave him for this "deviation." An idealist and a Slovak patriot, Clementis might conceivably have been the right man to rally the anti-Stalinist elements after the Soviet dictator's death if he had lived to see this event. His greatest enemy inside Czechoslovakia was Viliam Široký, who presented much of the case against Clementis at the trial and thereby got rid of a dangerous rival in Slovak as well as Czechoslovak politics.

While the judicial murder of Clementis was the more tragic event, not only for the man himself but also for his country, the fall and death of Slánský was the more ludicrous incident. Slánský, after all, had been an especially obsequious idolater of the Stalin image. Yet it was almost certainly Stalin who demanded his head, perhaps partly because Slánský had been rather close to Zhdanov, whose Russian protégés, too, fell after his death in August 1948. But there is no doubt that Slánský's Jewish origin, too, was a strong factor counting against him, and during the trial itself (when his name was frequently quoted in the press in its original, German-Jewish form of Salzmann) his own Jewishness and that of a number of other accused was extensively publicized. For Gottwald, Slánský's fall was certainly an advantage, as it buttressed his own position of power, now limited only by Moscow interference. Yet it is generally not assumed that Gottwald himself wanted to go as far as Stalin demanded and obtained. It can almost be considered a matter of course that both

Clementis and Slánský confessed to sinister crimes against the socialist society which they had never committed.

While the Czechoslovak regime tried, in the course of the 1950s, to catch up with other, neighboring regimes who had had more time to shape themselves after the Soviet image, the Stalinist group within the Polish government tried, with the help of Moscow, to fortify its position against a popular mood which was, to a large extent (very different from the Czechoslovak situation), basically anti-Russian. Moscow felt that it was necessary to do away with all elements within the party that were Polish enough to want at least a measure of autonomy for Poland.

Among those men who combined dedication to Communist ideas with a strong feeling for Poland by far the strongest personality was Władysław Gomułka. As the one man who could be expected to find some popular following, he was reluctantly accepted by the Kremlin as first secretary of the party, while three proved conformists were to balance the situation: Bolesław Bierut as president; Jakub Berman who played an important role in the secret police and was one of the most powerful men in the Polish Politbureau; and Hilary Minc, who was the chief economic planner. That Gomułka could stand up to the Stalinist triumvirate for three years was a tribute to his strong personality. It was owing to him, for instance, that wholesale confiscation and dismantling of factories and mines in the former East German territories—which were supposed to compensate Poland for her own eastern territories lost to the Soviet Union—was stopped after a bitter row. When, in a speech before the Central Committee of the Communist Party, he advocated an essentially autonomous policy for Poland, he was at first severely rebuked and forced to give up his post as secretary-general; then, in 1949, he was removed from the Central Committee, and two years later, in July 1951, was put behind prison bars. It appears possible that some extremely compromising secrets that Gomułka could have divulged prevented the regime from giving him a treatment comparable to that which Clementis underwent. If the Stalinist and "anti-Titoist" purge in Poland never reached extremes as bloody as in Czechoslovakia, Stalin nevertheless took steps designed to prevent any loosening of the fetters of his Polish dominion. The most spectacular step was the appointment, at the end of 1949, of a Marshal of the Soviet army, Konstantin Rokossovsky, as Polish minister of defense, commander in chief of Poland's armed forces, and a member of the Polish Politbureau. The fact that he had Polish ancestors did little to mitigate the humiliation this appointment imposed on Poland, particularly as a number of other high officers in commanding positions in Poland were Russians in Polish uniforms.

An issue that was sure to cause severe internal conflicts was the position of the church. Conflicts of this sort, in view of the claim of the Communist parties to be the sole shapers of the thoughts and beliefs of people, and especially young people, did of course arise in all of the Eastern European states within the Soviet orbit. In Czechoslovakia, for instance, the bishops of the Catholic church, including the Primate Archbishop Josef Beran, had either been interned or effectively muzzled by 1950. But Czechoslovakia, the country of Jan Hus, though Catholic in its majority, had always had strong non-Catholic minorities, and at least in the Western, Czech provinces there had long been a lively anticlerical tradition that made it somewhat easier for the new regime to find, among a considerable part of the population, if not allies at least neutral onlookers in its fight against the church. Not so in Poland. There the Church of Rome had, throughout much of the nation's history, played a special role and, in periods of conflict with Poland's two great neighbors, Roman Catholicism had seemed to identify true Polishness as against German Protestantism and Russian Orthodoxy. After World War II there were no religious minorities to speak of. The new government was aware that an impetuous proceeding against the church would be too unpopular, and would cause too sharp a reaction. Yet various ways were explored to weaken Catholic influence. A campaign to accuse the church of treason because Rome had as yet not confirmed a Polish church administration for the former German territories in the West met with limited success. But the organization of the so-called Patriot Priests was not successful in splitting and thus weakening the church. In 1950 the church, led by the Archbishop of Warsaw and Gniezno, Stephen Wyszyński, tried to prevent further difficulties by arranging a *modus vivendi* that included concessions from both sides. The government promised freedom of worship, the right to maintain religious education in schools, and freedom for a clerical press and for the functioning of religious orders, while the church gave assurances of support for the state, including its economic policy, and above all for the change of the provisional church administration into permanent Polish bishoprics in the western territories. However, the hope that on this basis there would be peace between state and church was to be disappointed. In September 1953, soon after having received the cardinal's hat, Archbishop Wyszyński was arrested. For a considerable time he was restricted to residence in an isolated monastery and prevented from fulfilling his official functions. Some other prelates also were imprisoned. But there never were any show trials such as those against the Catholic Primates in Budapest and Zagreb.

Stalin's death in 1953 had at first as little influence upon the situation in Poland as on that in Czechoslovakia. In both countries the Stalinist bureaucrats tried to dig themselves in all the more thoroughly. But in February 1956 Khrushchev's famous speech shook the belief in Stalin's infallibility and in the correctness of his policy not only in Russia but in most of the European countries within the Soviet orbit. In Poland this effect was strengthened by the fact that shortly after this revelation and the great attack upon the "cult of the individual," Poland's chief representative of Stalinist communism, Bolesław Bierut, died during a visit to Moscow. His successor, Edward Ochab, was chosen without—to some extent even against—Kremlin orders. It was a first step toward a certain degree of autonomy, and it called for more. The man considered as the worst Stalinist of all, Jakub Berman, was without much ado removed from the Politbureau. His disappearance made the secret police appear less frightening, and people began to speak up with more courage. The miserable standard of living of the people—at a moment when all available capital was still invested in heavy machinery and armaments—caused open resentment. Strike threats in Łódź were followed late in June by an open uprising in Poznań with strong anti-Russian undertones which led to fighting between the population, including tens of thousands of workers, and special security troops. Some were killed, many were arrested. The government, deeply embarrassed, tried to present the rising as inspired by Western capitalists. But it was soon clear that, if the regime wanted to avoid a more widespread rebellion—with the obvious danger of intervention by the

Soviet army still stationed on Polish territory—safety valves would have to be opened widely.

The solution that the majority of the party leadership—eventually including Ochab—accepted, in spite of the resistance of the so-called Natolin group, a clique of orthodox Stalinists firmly controlled by Soviet ambassador Ponomarenko, was to call back Gomułka to the leadership of the party. Gomułka laid down his conditions. One of the most important was the removal of Marshal Rokossovsky from the Politbureau and therewith also from any position of political power. This was too much for the Soviet government to take. In October, Moscow's top civilian and military leaders—Khrushchev, Molotov, Mikoyan, Kaganovich, Marshal Konev, and General Antonov—flew to Warsaw and insisted upon taking part in the decisive meeting of the Polish Politbureau. At the same time Russian troops began to move toward Warsaw.

For a moment it looked as if a violent explosion or complete Polish surrender were the only alternatives open. Supported not only by the party but by the great majority of the people, with a superb mixture of determination, coolness, and diplomatic moderation, Gomułka managed to avoid both these calamities. The Soviet troops were stopped, the Russian leaders returned to Moscow, the Natolin group was voted down (and largely out of their positions), and Rokossovsky returned to Russia. Cardinal Wyszyński was allowed to resume the duties of his office, and so were other leaders of the Catholic church. Another gain of the anti-Stalinist forces resulted from a speech by Gomułka in which he declared that it was up to the Polish farmers whether they wanted to belong to collective farms. As a result, 90 per cent of the 200,000 families which in 1955 had been pressured into such farms—even then a very small part of the total Polish peasantry—left the collectives. In 1957 only 21,000 families were left and this number has not changed much since—a situation that has been advantageous to Polish agriculture, especially in comparison with that of other countries of the Soviet orbit, including Czechoslovakia.

These results of what was—with the exception of Poznań—a peaceful and well directed anti-Stalinist revolution were remarkable enough and gave hope for an even greater measure of freedom to be achieved in the near future. This hope, however, was soon to shrink to much smaller dimensions than the people had expected. One reason for this was the outbreak of the Hungarian revolution and its bitter end. Only then the Polish people realized that they had by a hair's breadth escaped the danger of a catastrophe much like that suffered by the Hungarian rebels. It was this understanding that expressed itself in the outcome of the elections of 1957, when even the church, in a pastoral letter, came out openly for all believers to go to the polls and vote, at a moment when abstention (or the large-scale striking out of the names of Communist candidates) would have indicated opposition. In the outcome, the election—which in its methods was somewhat more representative than that of 1952—gave the Communists a small absolute majority.

The destruction of the Stalin myth by Khrushchev and the political earthquakes in Poland and Hungary did, of course, find echoes also in Czechoslovakia, but any attempts to follow in the traces of her neighbors to the north and south were quickly suppressed by the leaders of the ruling party. They had become so conditioned by the Stalinist atmosphere that they were even unwilling to accept fully the measure of de-Stalinization that had been started in the Soviet Union itself. Not only the potential representatives of Czechoslovak "national Communism" such as Clementis, but the very idea of such a movement seemed to have been killed by the great purge of 1951. As it became clear how Moscow reacted to the events in Poland, and especially in Hungary, the official party line in Prague turned as grimly critical of the new "Titoism" as it had been of the older, and a harsh Neo-Stalinism became the order of the day. For a while the borders between Czechoslovakia and Poland became almost as strong and effective a dividing line as that between Czechoslovakia and the West. President Zápotocký was essentially a cautious man who did not want to risk anything in moving away from the line prescribed by his predecessor. When he died in 1957, Antonín Novotný, who had since 1953 been the head of the Central Secretariat of the party, followed him in the presidency. He thus combined again the full power over party and government earlier held by Gottwald, and he wielded this power with determined rigidity.

Yet even the party and their leaders realized the need for a measure of internal change. This was perhaps most glaringly obvious in the relationship between the central government in Prague and the people of Slovakia. It was largely for that reason that the position of prime minister was put into the hands of a Slovak, Viliam Široký. As he was, however, the most vigorous representative of Neo-Stalinism among Slovak Communists, his rise to this high position by no means indicated any readiness of the Prague government to make real concessions to the wishes of the Slovak people.

The Slovaks had ample reason for complaint. An act passed by the Constituent Assembly in April 1946 had barred any constitutional changes concerning Slovakia except those approved by a majority of Slovak members, but this guaranty had been removed by the revised constitution imposed in May 1948. This was strongly resented by most Slovaks, including a large proportion of the members of the Slovak Communist Party, which has maintained, within the Czechoslovak party, a curious sort of semi-autonomy. In June 1956 some changes were made that, at least on paper, restored a few of the original rights granted in 1946 to the Slovak National Council, but these changes had little substance. A new constitution passed in July 1960 proclaimed not only Czechoslovakia as a socialist state but also laid down the principle of "democratic centralism." As all the real power rested with the central government and the Slovak National Council was hardly able to pass more than a handful of laws referring to economic and cultural issues, complaints continued to be heard, and were answered by Slovak Stalinists like Široký and the Slovak Communist Party's first secretary Bacílek with the accusation of "bourgeois nationalism" within the Slovak party. While, in purely economic terms, at least outside the agricultural sector, the situation in Slovakia had improved as a result of large industrial investments, in every other way the official condemnation of "Czechoslovakism" (the theory that Czechs and Slovaks are not two but one nation) seemed to change little in the actual relationship.

Yet the Slovak population, and especially its intelligentsia (as earlier in history), continued to play a role of considerable significance for the total development of the cultural and political atmosphere of the country. It was highly symptomatic that Laco Novomeský, a gifted writer and the most prominent "National Communist" among Slovak intellectuals, who at the time of the great purge had been expelled from the Writers' Union, was not only fully rehabilitated in 1963 but became one of the strongest and most influential voices for an effective de-Stalinization and liberalization of culture in Czechoslovakia. It was this movement that, in the same year, forced the reluctant Novotný to drop Prime Minister Široký (as well as Bacílek) and replace him with a young Slovak of the anti-Stalinist group, Josef Lenárt.

This liberalization, of course, did not go very far. On the other hand it was not limited to Slovakia but expressed itself also in Bohemia and Moravia, especially in Prague, where the removal of the colossal and oppressively ugly Stalin monument on the Letna hill above the Vltava river was a most characteristic symbolic action. Against the determined resistance of the elements favoring Stalinist reaction, slow but steady progress was made which at least narrowed, and to some extent removed, the distance by which Czechoslovakia had lagged behind the degree of relative freedom reached in Poland and even, after the immediate consequences of the events of 1956 had been overcome, in Hungary. The spiritual and intellectual Iron Curtain which had divided the Stalinist East from the Western world was pierced in many places. Western authors formerly banned (such as Hemingway) were translated and printed in substantial editions. Franz Kafka, long branded as a bourgeois, was not only reissued but became the center of long and appreciative public discussions. "Socialist Realism" was abandoned in painting and sculpture (where it had never made much of an imprint). Traveling, both into and out of Czechoslovakia, was made far easier, as had been done even earlier in Poland and Hungary. Early in 1965 Archbishop Beran, meanwhile promoted to Cardinal, was permitted to leave for Rome, and something like a compromise between church and state appeared to make the survival of Catholicism, if only under considerable restrictions, a possibility.

But all this can be evaluated as only a beginning. In relation to the liberalization, the general mellowing in the two West Slav countries, the rule seems to be that for every two steps forward, one step backward had to be made. Obviously no abandonment of some system of economic planning by the state should be expected; but a reform which tries to do away with the worst inadequacies of a rigidly bureaucratic and often incompetent management can be realistically hoped for, since the need for such a reform has been publicly admitted. It seems that, as long as no unforeseen developments occur, as long as the great internal discussion in the Communist world continues and as long as the reduction of tension in Soviet-American relations continues, there will be no complete reversal of the direction away from Stalinism, toward a more mature, more humane, and to some extent more representative organization of public life. This would also allow a better understanding between East Central Europe and the Western world with which these countries have had such close and determining ties all through their long, colorful, and often tragic history.

TWO

The West Slavs in the Middle Ages

Czechoslovakia and Poland are close neighbors, joined by a long—in European terms, very long—border, nearly 400 miles as the crow flies and about half as long again if measured in detail, much longer than, say, the borders between France and Germany or France and Spain. Czechoslovakia and Poland, with Hungary added, form what is generally called East Central Europe. One might assume that, belonging to the same limited region of Europe, their geography, too, would be somewhat similar.

Nothing could be farther from the truth. In terms of physical geography, they share only the mountains that also separate them: the Sudeten chain in the western part, the Carpathians (containing the beautifully alpine High Tatra) in the eastern part. Otherwise few countries sharing a limited region could be more different.

Poland occupies a central section of the great plain that covers the northern part of continental Europe and that reaches from the Atlantic (north of the Bay of Biscay) to the Ural mountains, becoming ever wider as it opens out toward the east. In this plain all rivers west of Russia flow in a northwesterly direction toward the English Channel, the North Sea, and the Baltic Sea, but none of the rivers forms a true natural border. Not even the wide lower Rhine has ever been a true natural border, separating peoples or civilizations. As a consequence, all through history nations and states have moved east and west across this plain as if swaying with the wind—French, Germans, Poles, Lithuanians, and Russians. The Poles, perhaps, were worse off than the others. Though in the Middle Ages they themselves engaged in expansion and developed a sort of "Drang nach Osten" ("urge toward the East") not unlike the early eastward movement of the Germans, they have been pushed around to a greater extent than any other of Europe's major nations. There is little doubt that geography had something to do with it, making those shifts appear easy to Poland's neighbors and, as far as Polish expansion was concerned, to the Poles themselves. There is, it is true, the valley of the Vistula which, except for the very earliest times, has always been something like a Polish heartland. Both Cracow, a former capital, and Warsaw, the present capital, lie on the shores of this river. But east and west of it there were vast changes. Warsaw, which throughout much of her history was distinctly in the western region of Poland, is now just as distinctly in the eastern region, merely 100 miles from the nearest Soviet border, but almost 300 from that of East Germany. Apart from the mountains to the south and the coast in the north, the various regions of the country are basically similar, with sluggish rivers meandering across the plain, although there are some great lakes and forests mainly in the northeast, which was the southern part of East Prussia until 1945.

In contrast, there is no lack of natural borders in the case of Czechoslovakia. This is especially true for the westernmost part, Bohemia, the province which in earlier times, as the Kingdom of Bohemia, had been the main part of the realm of the Crown of St. Wenceslas. Bohemia, with its diamond shape, can easily be traced on a purely physical map, as her borders run mostly on the crest of the surrounding mountain ranges, the Bohemian Forest (Šumava) to the southwest, the various mountain regions now called the Sudeten Mountains to the northwest and northeast, and the Moravian Heights to the southeast. Within these borders lies a rich and remarkably diverse country, with great forests, old volcanic hills, fertile plains, winding rivers, and many (mostly man-made) lakes, a continent within a continent, as Goethe put it after one of his frequent visits to western Bohemia. Neighboring Moravia, like Bohemia predominantly inhabited by people of Czech ancestry and language, is also surrounded by ranges of mountains and hills except in the south, where it opens up to the Danube Basin. Moravia's borders, with few exceptions, also run on the crests of mountains or hills and create a distinct and unified, if in many ways diverse and rich, image, somewhat softer and milder, with fewer contrasts, than the greater sister to the west. To the southeast Moravia leads into the easternmost of Czechoslovakia's three natural divisions, Slovakia. The southwestern section of Slovakia, the region along the Danube and the lower courses of its tributaries Váh, Nitra, and Hron, is flat, belonging in physical geography to the great central Danubian plain whose greater part is occupied by Hungary, whereas the more characteristic northern regions are mountainous. The Slovaks, to a considerable part, are mountain people; their language—which is rather softer and more melodious than the closely related Czech—has many dialects, almost as many as there are valleys. In contrast to the Poles and the Czechs, the Slovaks, as a national entity conscious of their nationhood, have never had a state quite their own prior to 1918, but lived for nearly 900 years within the framework of the Hungarian kingdom. Until Hungary turned to a fervent and uncompromising Magyar nationalism in the nineteenth century, the Slovaks had something like a steady home in this multinational state where Latin was the official language. The Czechs, on the other hand, had been among the first Slavic nations to develop a state, within borders much like those of today, even though they were never, until quite recently, in the sole possession of the whole of their country—or their two countries, Bohemia and Moravia. While they were never shifted around on the map of Europe, they had to manage to exist in a difficult symbiosis with people belonging, in descent and language, to their greatest and most influential but in some ways also most dangerous neighbor, the Germans. The same, however, was true to a somewhat lesser extent for Poland.

EARLY HISTORY

There was, in the earliest history or prehistory of the West Slavs, a time when there was as yet little clear differentiation between Poles, Czechs, and Slovaks, and when besides them some other Slavic tribes belonged, at least linguistically and probably also ethnically, to the same group. As did the other Slavonic peoples, they seem to have come from an earlier region of settlement north and east of the Carpathian Mountains, much of which later became Poland. The plains farther to the west were inhabited, at the beginning of the Middle Ages, by the Polabians (Elbe-Slavs), who actually reached far west beyond the Elbe, the Lusatian Serbs or Wends in the territory just north of Bohemia, and the Pomeranians in the territories along the Baltic (hence the name Pomerania, from *po morze*—by the sea coast), the last group closely related to the Poles. Only a small number of Wends—less than 150,000—are still in existence today, in the former Margravate of Lusatia now belonging to East Germany; they speak a language close to both Czech and Polish. All other West Slav tribal groups in this region that are neither Polish nor Czech or Slovak were, in the course of the Middle Ages, Germanized or, to a lesser extent, Polonized. (Whether a very early civilization now called Lusatian, which had existed in the West Slav territories prior to 500 B.C., was actually a Slavic one is not yet fully determined, though many arguments seem to confirm this theory.)

The Slavic settlement of the territories south of the mountain chain probably did not occur till the fifth century A.D. Much of these lands had, for some time, been occupied by a Celtic tribe, the Boii, whose name has gone into that of Bohemia as well as that of its southwestern neighbor, Bavaria. They were followed by the Germanic tribes of the Marcomanni and Quadi, but these tribes soon migrated south and west and left Bohemia open to the immigration of the Slavs. The theory presented by some German historians of Bohemia that the later German population in the country presents a residuum from an original German population has in recent times been disproved by Czech and German scholars.

The earliest Slavs in Central Europe had a rather loose tribal organization, unable to withstand the invasions on the part of Asiatic peoples such as the Huns and later their relatives, the Avars. For a while—throughout the second half of the sixth century—the Avars dominated most of Central and East Central Europe and its large Slavic population. Early in the seventh century, however, the Slavic people of part of East Central Europe, comprising most of today's Czechoslavakia, the eastern part of Austria, and the territory between the Elbe and the Saale called "White Serbia," rebelled and freed themselves from Avar rule. They were led by a man called Samo, believed to have been a merchant prince or nobleman, probably of Frankish origin, who established himself firmly as lord over a large territory and even managed to defeat an army sent by the Frankish King Dagobert—a feat possible only on the basis of a relatively well organized political body. Yet at his death in 658 or 659, after a long reign of 35 years, Samo's empire, the first distinctly Slavic state, disappeared from history and there are no further traces of it.

The Moravian Empire

The center of Samo's state seems to have been in Moravia. While this location is only a probability, it is a certainty in the case of the next development of a similar nature—the rise of the state generally called the Moravian (or Greater Moravian) Empire. While we do not know much of its beginnings—there may even have been a connection with Samo's empire—we do know that its first strong ruler, Mojmir I, having probably accepted Christianity from the Bishop of Passau, had by 830 united several Slavic tribes and gained practical independence for this state from the Frankish Empire to the West. In particular, Mojmir resented the intrusion of the Roman clergy from southern Bavaria, which had developed under the protection of the early Carolingian emperors. About 833 he drove the Slavic prince Pribina from his residence at Nitra in Slovakia, where Pribina had allowed a church to be built and consecrated by the Archbishop of Salzburg. Pribina then, with Frankish permission, established himself for a while in central Hungary (Pannonia). The Moravian state grew under Mojmir and especially under his son and successor Rastislav (846-70), it spread to the east into the Pannonian plain, where before the midcentury it reached the Tisza river, the westernmost border of the great contemporary empire of the Bulgars, and to the north, where it began to include territories beyond the Carpathians. This Moravian empire, which eventually, for a relatively short period, included also the Slavs inhabiting Bohemia, is generally considered to have been the earliest state in which the ancestors of Czechs and Slovaks lived together within one political framework. To make, for that time, a clear distinction between the two groups is difficult, if not impossible. Neither language nor any other criterion can clearly determine whether the inhabitants of Moravia and present-day Slovakia were Czechs or Slovaks in the ninth century. At a much later date—indeed, in modern times—many Moravians preferred to consider themselves as "Moravané" rather than "Češi," although there were neither ethnic nor language differences. The claim made by some modern Slovak writers that the Moravian Empire of the ninth century was really and exclusively "the old kingdom of the Slovaks" has hardly more historical justification than the rather similar theory that early Kievan Russia was really a Ukrainian rather than a Russian state and civilization. But that the Old Moravians had, among themselves, substantial numbers destined to become the ancestors of the Slovaks cannot be doubted, and the Great Moravian tradition later became an important element in the development of modern Slovak nationalism.

The Moravian state had seen, at its very beginnings, a lively spread of Christianity, and modern archeology has discovered a large number of church buildings of that period. But under Rastislav a further important step was taken. In agreement with the policy of his father, who had feared and resented Frankish claims of overlordship, even if based on ecclesiastical administration, Rastislav decided about 860 to receive missionaries from the more distant and less threatening Byzantine Empire. His need for support from there was increased by the fact that he was under pressure from the large territory separating the Moravian realm from Byzantium, the young Empire of the Bulgars—not originally Slavic—under its great ruler Boris I. Boris' position in regard to Byzantium was somewhat similar to Rastislav's relationship with the Frankish Empire. Boris had for that reason begun to negotiate with Rome on the acceptance of western clergy, and with Louis the German on an alliance that would have been directed against Moravia. Around 860 Rastislav, feeling that only a Byzantine alliance could safeguard his position, sent an embassy to Constantinople asking Emperor Michael III for the dispatch of churchmen able to speak the Slav language and to fortify still more firmly his people's Christianity. The request was granted with the arrival in Moravia, in 863, of the two great "Apostles of the Slavs," the brothers Constantine (later called Cyril) and Methodius, both of whom were eventually sainted.

These men were Greeks from the half-Slavic province of Thessalonica. Constantine-Cyril, a brilliant linguist, used the Slavic dialect of Macedonia for the development of a written language (later known as Old Church Slavonic) and of an alphabet which was known as Glagolitic and whose later development, called Cyrillic after him, was to become the alphabet of all Slavs who embraced the Greek Orthodox religion, notably all Russians, but also Bulgarians, Macedonians, and Serbs.

The work of the brothers was, at first, most successful. In spite of the opposition of the German bishops of Regensburg and Passau their activities, including the introduction of a Slavonic liturgy, were supported by Pope Nicholas I. He invited the brothers to Rome (where Cyril died), and his successor Adrian II appointed Methodius to be archbishop of a restored archdiocese of Pannonia, which was to include all of the lands of the Moravian Empire. The position of Methodius was endangered, however, by political developments in Moravia. In 870 Prince Svatopluk, a nephew of Rastislav, rebelled against his uncle, allying himself with the Franks under Louis the German. Rastislav was captured, blinded, and imprisoned, and for a short while Louis held sway over the Moravian realm. Then Svatopluk, an unscrupulous but highly gifted soldier and administrator, turned against his German allies and protectors and in a series of engagements threw them out of the country. In 874 Louis acknowledged, in a peace treaty signed at Forchheim, the independence of the Moravian state with the exception of an annual payment of tribute. During the following two decades of his reign, Svatopluk extended his rule over Bohemia, the later March of Meissen, all of Silesia, and much of the upper Vistula valley, including western and central Galicia. In the south, Svatopluk's empire included much of central Hungary, probably down to the Drava river.

The existence of so large and powerful a state in the path of their own desired eastward expansion was strongly resented by the East Franks, and their ruler, Arnulf, a grandson of Louis the German, tried as early as 892 to weaken the Moravian realm by allying himself with the nomadic Magyars. The Magyars, however, were at this time still engaged in a difficult struggle with Boris of Bulgaria. As long as Svatopluk lived, the attempts of his enemies in east and west came to nothing, and one of Arnulf's strongest armies was, in 893, completely destroyed by an army of Moravians, Czechs from Bohemia, and Lusatian Serbs. In 894, however, Svatopluk died, and his successor Mojmir II had to fight not only foreign enemies but also the claims of two brothers over part of the heritage. Under these conditions the empire began to crumble. As early as 895 some princes from Bohemia defected to the Frankish side. In the same year the bulk of the Magyar migration, led by the great Árpád, crossed the Carpathian passes from the east into the Pannonian plain. In the following year the alliance between them and Arnulf against the Moravians was renewed. Around 900 the Moravian holdings in Pannonia were lost to the Magyars. The unequal struggle against Germans and Magyars lasted a few years, but in a final battle, probably in 907, Mojmír II fell and his realm succumbed.

The fall of the Greater Moravian Empire and the establishment of the Magyars in the central plain on both sides of the Danube and Tisza rivers had an enormous significance for further European development. Since the Magyars—after fierce fights with the Germans, who had reason to regret having called them in—eventually settled as far west as the borders of the Bavarian East Marches, the later Austria, a wedge was driven between West and South Slavs at a time when the latter, too, especially the Croats of Dalmatia, had begun to develop their own civilization and political organization. The differences between these two branches of the Slavic world, West and South, had not been great until then; they did become more marked as a result of the geographic separation. But with it went also a separation between the West Slavs and the Eastern church centered in the capital of the Byzantine Empire. The church of Methodius, indeed, had already encountered great difficulties during the reign of Svatopluk, who considered it politically wiser to reconcile the German clergy, and the great apostle had even been imprisoned by the Bavarian bishops and only released upon the indignant protest of Pope John VIII. After the death of Methodius in 884 his Frankish successor, long his enemy, exiled the Saint's disciples, who were received with open arms in Bulgaria and Dalmatia; from these lands the Slavic liturgy eventually was able to conquer not only the great majority of the Balkan Slavs but also Russia when that country, toward the turn of the millennium, accepted Christianity. A smaller number of Methodius' disciples went to Bohemia, where the Slavonic ritual, on a modest scale, survived till the eleventh century.

The Moravian Empire was, in a sense, only an episode in the history of the West Slavs, and especially of Czechs and Slovaks. But it did influence, as a live tradition, the later attitudes of their descendants. Recent archaeological research, still in full swing, has shown the economic and cultural level of Moravia in the ninth century to have been much further advanced than had originally been assumed, with a distinctly structured society and with organized, defendable settlements of considerable size, places deserving the names of towns or cities and containing numbers of easily recognizable church buildings. Clearly the old Moravians, with a tradition of trade with Byzantium and with quite sophisticated crafts in ceramics, metals, and other fields, had developed far beyond the level of their Magyar conquerors, and also beyond that of their closest relatives, the Czechs of Bohemia, to whom, after the Moravian catastrophe, the leadership of the West Slavs south of the mountains was now to fall.

Bohemia

The beginnings of the history of Bohemia proper go back to a period in which the borders between myth and fact are somewhat nebulous. The term "Czechs," which gave its name also to the country (in Czech, *Čechy*), originally referred only to one of a number of Slavic tribes in Bohemia, one which had its main settlements in the region of Prague and which slowly gained the upper hand. Its princes, the Přemyslid dynasty, which was destined to rule over the country for more than 400 years, claimed descent from Přemysl, the plowman whom the great princess Libuše (or Libussa) called from his lowly work to the throne. The list of his descendants through earlier times is largely fictitious until it reaches the second half of the ninth century with Duke Bořivoj who, according to an old tradition, received baptism from Methodius himself. He seems, indeed, to have built the first churches in the country. With the rapid weakening of the Moravian state after Svatopluk's death two Czech princes, aware of the impossibility to stem by themselves the Magyar invasion, promised their allegiance to the Frankish Empire at a *Reichstag* at Regensburg in 895. This western-directed policy, as well as further Christianization, was purposefully continued by Bořivoj's widow Ludmilla and especially by his grandson Wenceslas (Václav) who, however, was murdered in 929 at the instigation of his brother Boleslav. The national legend made him a martyr to his faith, and as Bohemia's national saint (and the "Good King Wenceslas" of the English carol) his magic name has wielded great influence upon Czech thought and history.

Duke Boleslav, like his brother, was a Christian, and his bloody act, never properly explained, probably had personal and political rather than religious motives. He was a powerful and ambitious man and did a great deal to consolidate the Czech state, even though a part of eastern Bohemia enjoyed a sort of autonomy under another princely family, the Slavníks. With their cooperation Boleslav I managed to restore much if not most of the former Moravian empire. He added to Bohemia the later Margravate of Moravia (largely within its eventual borders), most of what is now Slovakia, much of Silesia, and the territory around Cracow. The eastern territories, especially those north of the Danube valley, had at that time not yet become firmly occupied by the Hungarians, who were still trying to penetrate westward toward and into Bavaria. With the effective help of a strong Czech contingent under Boleslav's personal leadership, Otto I, the second German king of the Saxon dynasty and later the restorer of the Western Roman Empire, succeeded in the great Battle of the Lechfeld (955) in defeating and bringing to a halt the Magyar westward expansion. Boleslav's policy was thus directed toward combining friendly relationships with the German king, even at the cost of mainly formal feudal ties, with a systematic strengthening of his own realm.

Poland and Moravia

It was quite within the framework of this policy that Boleslav I, toward the later period of his long reign—he died in 967—initiated a policy of close cooperation with the leader of the other West Slav state, Poland. In 965 he gave his daughter in marriage to the Polish prince, Mieszko. This is the first official confrontation of the two West Slav states, which thus began, but did not long continue, on a happy note of friendship and alliance in the face of the overwhelming power of the common western neighbor. It also was at least symbolic of Mieszko's decision to accept Christianity for himself and his people.

Mieszko's beginnings are unknown. He is supposed to have descended, in the fourth generation, from a mythical figure named

Piast, who was, like Přemysl, originally a peasant. (It is perhaps characteristic that both these famous ancient royal houses that were to rule the two nations through most of the Middle Ages proclaimed their pride in descent from a tiller of the soil.)

As in the earlier case of the Moravian Empire, the issue of the ecclesiastical administration of the new Slavic states immediately assumed great significance. The two princes acted in unison, asking Pope John XIII (965-72) to grant them the right to establish bishoprics. The Pope was willing as long as Emperor Otto I was in agreement. On this basis bishoprics were founded in both countries, in Poznań and Prague. The Polish See was put directly under Rome (Mieszko later—about 990—in a symbolic gesture declared his whole realm to be tributary to the Papacy), while the bishopric of Prague was put under the Archbishopric of Mainz. The choice of Mainz may have been made in agreement with the Czech ruler, since this faraway metropolis would not be as inclined to mingle in interior Bohemian affairs as would Magdeburg or Salzburg, both of which had tried hard to achieve a sort of monopoly in expanding German ecclesiastical influence eastward. Nevertheless the fact that Prague was under a German archbishop underlined a dependence which was absent in the case of Poznań. In due time this would make it easier for Poland to shake off the degree of feudal overlordship that the Saxon and Salic emperors claimed and generally managed to maintain over both West Slav states.

This was all the easier for them as the two states, toward the end of Mieszko's reign and under his son and successor Bolesław I, called Chrobry (the Brave), drifted apart, partly at least because the Slavník princes, unwilling to let the Prague dukes grow too strong, had tried to put themselves under Polish protection. This also led to an alienation between Boleslav II and the second bishop of Prague, Adalbert or Vojtěch, himself one of the Slavník princes. Adalbert was an extraordinary and powerful religious personality who took a hand in the widening and deepening of Christian teaching not only in his own Czech lands but also in Hungary and Poland. He was friend and mentor to the young, highly gifted, and impressionable Emperor Otto III (983-1002). Banished from Prague, Adalbert went first to Rome and then, via Poland, proceeded on a northward mission during which he was martyred in 997 by the heathen Prussians. His body was brought back to Poland and buried in Gniezno, at that time Poland's capital.

The Emperor agreed that an archbishopric should be established at the burial place of his old friend, who was almost immediately canonized, and in March 1000 was present himself at that solemn event. He also confirmed his prior policy, which was to give the Slavic states as well as other European nations a status of almost complete autonomy in a sort of federally organized empire with the center in Rome. It was a grandiose conception of a nationally diverse yet politically and religiously united Europe, often criticized as fantastic by German historians, and perhaps, indeed, beyond realization at the time, especially since the great Emperor, son of a Saxon father and a Byzantine mother, died two years later.

After his death it was at first assumed in both West Slav countries that they would have to take a place on the European stage as members of a Roman Empire with its present center in Germany but closely tied to the Roman church, and that they themselves would have to play an important role in it. Bolesław the Brave initially recognized Otto's successor Henry II as Emperor, but conflicts broke out very soon, especially over Bohemia.

Bolesław's enterprise against his southern neighbor was mainly caused by a great slaughter in which his mother's brother, Boleslav II, had killed most of the members and attendants of the princely house of Slavník after a siege of their castle of Libice. The only survivor fled to the court of Bolesław the Brave. When Boleslav II died and the much weaker but tyrannical Boleslav III succeeded him, the Polish ruler invaded Bohemia and in 1003 conquered Prague, where he was received with joy. For a moment the vision of a united West Slav empire, comparable to Greater Moravia but now under Polish guidance, appeared on the horizon, but it was a vision which the new Emperor Henry II did not enjoy. With a strong army he drove the Poles from Prague and reinstated the Přemyslid Jaromír, a brother of Boleslav III, upon the throne. The hope for a united Slavic empire was shattered, but Bolesław the Brave still came out of the struggle with notable gains. He retained Silesia, the region of Cracow, much of Moravia, and most of Slovakia. He also, in one victorious eastern campaign, gained Galician territories and even entered

Kiev. Several attempts by the Emperor to reduce him to obedience and destroy the newly risen east-European great power met with failure. It was certainly an appropriate gesture when, at Christmas 1024, only some months before his death, Bolesław could, with papal approval, have a royal crown put on his head.

This step had great significance. It was a deliberate challenge to the claims of the Holy Roman Empire and its Emperor to include the territories of the east as tributaries and vassals. It was understood in this sense also by the German ruling groups. While it had proved impossible, at this stage, to destroy Poland as a strong independent power, it seemed all the more necessary to prevent Bohemia from becoming too strong. German interests were well served by the fact that Czech succession was based on the principle of the seniorate, which was bound to cause trouble between members of the ducal house. Repeatedly some of them would appeal to the Emperor for a decision on the distribution of land and power. As long as there was the fear of a strong and expansive Polish kingdom to the north, seemingly eager to swallow the Czech lands, some Czech princes would feel the need to accept German protection and overlordship. Yet the strong minds among Czech princes, like their Polish peers, thought in terms of an independent policy.

Polish princes, too, became victims of internal dynastic struggles before long. This occurred soon after the great Bolesław's death. His quite able successor, Mieszko II, was deprived of part of his heritage by a dissatisfied brother and, under strong pressure from both Germany and Kievan Russia (which, under Yaroslav the Wise, had just reached the zenith of its early history), finally resigned his claim to kingship in 1033. (Here much later developments threw their first shadows.) While Poland seemed to grow ever weaker under Mieszko's successors, the Czech Duke Břetislav I, called the Restorer, proceeded to regain what had earlier been lost to Poland. In two great campaigns he not only won back all of Moravia, which from then on remained firmly tied to Bohemia, but also reconquered Silesia and Cracow and occupied Poznań and Gniezno. He then transferred the body of Saint Adalbert from the seat of Poland's archbishops to his own bishop's seat, Prague. However, Břetislav's hope that this act would induce the Holy See to elevate Prague, like Gniezno, to the rank of an archbishopric was disappointed. Břetislav's goal was essentially King Bolesław's dream of a united West Slav power, merely translated from Polish into Czech. In either language it seemed unbearable to the Emperor Henry III. A powerful armed invasion forced Břetislav to evacuate Poland except for Silesia which, however, went back to Poland some years later under the condition of a yearly tribute to be paid to Bohemia.

Břetislav still hoped to regain at least Slovakia which had, under Bolesław the Brave, come into Polish possession but had been lost soon after his death, in 1026, to Stephen I of Hungary. Břetislav therefore took part in three campaigns that the Emperor waged against King Andrew I of Hungary, which proved abortive. From then on, except for some small Slovak border regions that temporarily came under Polish rule, the land of the Slovaks remained part of the Kingdom of Hungary until 1918.

In Poland, Casimir, the son of Mieszko II, after suppressing a wave of pagan reaction against the church, tried to restore health and cohesion to his country by carefully avoiding any challenge to German suzerainty. But Casimir's son Bolesław (1058-79) consciously followed in the footsteps of his great ancestor whose name he bore and amply deserved the epithet "the Bold." His great opportunity came with the development of the conflict between imperial and papal claims culminating in the Investiture Struggle. Bolesław II supported the papal side throughout, sometimes quite effectively and to the great satisfaction of Pope Gregory VII. As a consequence he was able, late in his reign, on Christmas Day 1076, just a few days before the humble appearance of Henry IV at Canossa, to be crowned king of Poland by the Archbishop of Gniezno. Bolesław II undertook many actions that, he hoped, would profit Poland indirectly, by weakening the Empire, and directly, by adding to Poland's territories. In Hungary, especially, he interfered with great effort, expenditure, and success, replacing Andrew I and his son Solomon, brother-in-law of both Emperor Henry IV and of the Czech Duke Vratislav II, with his own, and Pope Gregory's, candidates. As a result the long-sustained German claim to suzerainty over Hungary finally lapsed with the reign of St. Ladislas I. Far less successful was Bolesław II in his ambitious attempts to impose upon Kievan Russia a ruler ready for religious reunion with Rome.

While Bolesław's projects and acts clearly show greatness and consistency of political vision, they also suggest an expending of the country's strength which probably went beyond its economic capacity or at least beyond the willingness of the increasingly powerful feudal nobility to support the king's costly enterprises. When, in 1079, the king ordered the cruel execution, supposedly for treason, of Bishop Stanisław of Cracow, who soon became Poland's patron saint, a rebellion of the nobility drove him from the country. His successor, Władysław Hermann, dropped the claim to the rank of king, which was not renewed in Poland for more than two centuries. This was merely a symbol of a policy of relative weakness, equally in relation to the German imperial power, which Władysław supported fully, and to the power of the feudal nobility, temporal as well as ecclesiastical.

The Czech reigning prince of the time, like the Polish, was deeply involved in the struggles between Empire and Papacy. Duke Vratislav II proved himself a worthy son of Břetislav but of a less romantic, more realistic nature. He managed to support Henry IV throughout his long wars, especially against Rudolf of Suabia, the "Anti-King," a struggle in which Czech support proved decisive. Yet he still maintained at least a tolerably good relationship with Pope Gregory VII, thus making sure that the struggle would not, as it did in Germany, result in a deep rift within the country. The reward Vratislav hoped for and requested had a twofold character—acquisition of the Marches of Meissen and Lusatia for Bohemia, and a royal crown. In the first Vratislav was disappointed. The second he received from Henry at a solemn synod at Mainz in April 1085. It seems remarkable that the first Czech prince to become a king did so just six years after the last of the early Polish kings had been dethroned, and indeed the two events are clearly interconnected, for Henry bestowed upon Vratislav the title "King of Bohemia and Poland." Vratislav made no use of his Polish title, was generally on good terms with his neighbor and son-in-law Władysław, and probably had never asked for this double kingship. In fact, it was clearly a demonstration on the part of the Emperor, intending to show that it was up to him and not to the Pope to make kings, especially within the orbit claimed by the Empire.

Yet it would be quite wrong to consider Vratislav's kingship an empty title. His enthroning was an important break in the tradition of the Holy Roman Empire, within which there had been no king beside the *Rex Romanorum* who, it is true, was also *Rex Teutonicus* and, at times, *Rex Italicus*, but always the one person whom papal coronation could make Emperor. This tradition—with the exception of the Bohemian kingship—remained unbroken through the centuries; even in the early eighteenth century the Elector of Brandenburg could become king only in his Prussian duchy, which was outside the Empire. All through these centuries the King of Bohemia was to be the only one who, while still enfeoffed with his dignity by the Emperor, would stand at his side as another anointed and crowned king. It would put him far above all other princes within the Empire. By reaching this first step—the personal kingship, not yet hereditary—Vratislav started on the very special, very singular way in which the Czech commonwealth established its position half inside and half outside the Holy Roman Empire—inside in that its rulers played an increasingly important role in the development of imperial policy, outside in that the possibility of the Emperor to interfere, as supreme feudal lord, in the internal affairs of Bohemia and her dependencies was always small and could be systematically whittled down till nothing was left of it. The Czech policy, which was willing to go the road of compromise between complete independence and participation as a member state within the Holy Roman Empire, was often criticized, especially by Polish historians, who regarded this compromise as a sign of weakness and a sin against West Slav solidarity. But it must not be forgotten that, unlike Poland, Bohemia was always surrounded on three sides by German territories, and furthermore that the Holy Roman Empire itself was far from a centralized nation-state and became more and more a loose confederacy of essentially sovereign principalities and city states. In this framework Bohemia could increasingly play a predominant role and thus be, in her strongest periods, a Central European power of remarkable political vitality and cultural significance.

CONSOLIDATION AND GREATNESS

During the high Middle Ages the two West Slav states, and Hungary with her strong Slovak population in the north, belonged to the world of European feudalism. A measure of social differentiation can be observed already in the civilization of Greater Moravia, and for the early societies of Bohemia and Poland the early claim that they had been primitive rural democracies has long been abandoned by modern historians. Of the two states Bohemia was, in the time of the earlier Přemyslids and Piasts, economically more highly developed, both in agriculture and in the growth of the crafts. In both countries, but to a larger extent in Bohemia, German colonization played a considerable role, although a good deal of colonizing activity, especially the clearing of forests, was done also by Slavic settlers. German legal forms of hereditary tenure were widespread and became instrumental in activating Slavic peasant settlement as much as that of German immigrants. Germans, called in by the princes, also functioned as "locatores" in the founding and development of towns which, however, except for Prague, began to play an important role only in the thirteenth century. At that time Bohemia turned into one of the great town regions of Europe, to some extent comparable with parts of Italy, Flanders, and Western Germany.

The prime movers in bringing about the strong development of self-governing towns in Bohemia were the kings of the Přemyslid dynasty. For them the cities were both a valuable source of taxation and a possible basis of support in their defense against baronial antagonism. One of the most important steps in the strengthening of the monarchy in Bohemia—at a time when this institution underwent a prolonged period of weakness in Poland—was the change-over from the original seniority system to primogeniture. The seniority system, by putting on the throne the eldest member of the dynasty, only too frequently led to fierce quarrels among contestant princes and gave both the Emperor and the domestic nobility opportunities to interfere and weaken the central power of the monarch. The last of those epochs of domestic wars occurred in Bohemia at the end of the reign of Vladislav II who, in 1158, received the royal crown (as King Vladislav I) from Emperor Frederick I as a reward for his help in the Italian wars. But Vladislav could not immediately pass the crown on to his heirs because of the fierce struggle between them. Eventually, however, his son Přemysl I Otakar gained the crown in 1198 as an indubitably hereditary institution. The constitutional basis for this change was laid more firmly by the Golden Bull of Sicily, issued in 1212 by Emperor Frederick II, whose universal recognition over Otto IV in Germany had owed much to Přemysl's support. This Golden Bull reduced the duties owed by the King of Bohemia to the Empire to a very minimum. The king was expected to take part in imperial court days only if those were held in a city near the Bohemian border and was to send no more than 300 horse (or, if he chose, contribute 300 marks of silver) to the Roman coronation campaign of the Emperor. The Emperor on his part waived all claims to the right of interference in the Bohemian succession, except for the mere formality of confirming the choice of the Czechs themselves. This, in fact, meant the right of the great nobles to elect one of the king's sons. Largely owing to the fact that for several generations during the thirteenth century only one son survived his father, the institution of primogeniture, independent of the wishes of the nobility, established itself firmly in Bohemia. As most of the Přemyslid kings were vigorous personalities, sure of their purposes, and had considerable incomes (for example, from the rich silver mines of Bohemia), their position in relation to the nobility was strengthened. So, also, was their position vis-à-vis the Empire in which they enjoyed great influence without being subject to any imperial control. Imperial law had no validity in the Bohemian realm, the king issued his own money, and he had the right to invest the bishops of Bohemia and Moravia. Earlier attempts of German rulers, especially Frederick I, to transform Moravia into a direct fief of the Empire were given up, and the Moravian Margravate remained, from then on, firmly tied to Bohemia.

The strength thus gained by the crown in cooperation with the cities founded during the reigns of Wenceslas I (1230-54) reached its peak under Wenceslas' son Přemysl Otakar II (1254-78), the most brilliant of the Czech kings of his century. He was not only unusually successful in the economic strengthening of Bohemia and Moravia (especially through the further development of cities), but also, at least for a time, in his endeavor to expand the possessions of the Bohemian crown. In his time a close relationship developed between some of the Silesian princes of the Piast dynasty, especially the prince of Breslau (Wrocław, Vratislav) and the court of Prague. He also supported the Teutonic knights in a crusade resulting in the founding of the city of Königsberg, named after him. More important was the fact that upon the extinction of the male line of the Austrian ducal house of Babenberg the Czech king took possession of the duchies of Austria, Styria, Carinthia, and Carniola. He successfully defended those southern possessions and, with the acquisition of the Patriarchate of Aquileia, he pushed down to the Adriatic Sea, against the competing claims of Stephen V of Hungary. He achieved much for the internal development of these territories during his reign there. For a while it seemed that, in view of the desolate conditions in the Empire after the fall of the Hohenstaufen dynasty, Přemysl would have the best chance to gain the imperial crown as well, but the very extent of his territorial power (and the favor he showed the cities) antagonized the German princes, who preferred Rudolf, Count of Hapsburg, a little known if experienced and well-to-do member of the imperial nobility. Rudolf was also supported by the Hungarian king and by some of the great Czech barons, who disliked the growth of royal power. Fighting for his heritage in two wars Přemysl fell, in 1278, at Dürnkrut (near the Marchfeld). The battle established the Hapsburgs for many centuries in the Austrian territories, though the expansionist tendencies of the late Přemyslids did not yet end. They now included Bohemia's great northern neighbor, Poland.

Poland had, in the twelfth and thirteenth centuries, suffered from the same evil that had, throughout most of the twelfth century, weakened Bohemia: the seniority system. But while its effects in Bohemia had in the main been limited to dynastic struggles, the more dangerous result for Poland was the loss of her unity. It was Bolesław III (called Wrymouth, 1102-38) who—after a generally successful reign in which he was able to annex western Pomerania—in his will divided his country into separate parts under his sons—an act which led to the establishment of nearly independent territories in Silesia, Great Poland, Little Poland (with Cracow), and Masovia. The ruling that the senior prince, as grand duke, should maintain a role of paramountcy was not effective. Bolesław IV (1146-73) as grand duke was forced by Emperor Frederick Barbarossa to acknowledge Poland's position as a fief of the Empire. At the same time the weakness of the princes and the lack of national unity (maintained only in ecclesiastical organization) gave the nobility the chance to strengthen its hold over much of the country. Even more dangerous for Poland, at least in the long run, was the appeal of one of the Piast princes, Conrad of Masovia, to the recently established Order of the Teutonic Knights for help in the defense of his duchy against the heathen Prussians. In the years from 1228 to 1233, the Knights' Grand Master, Hermann of Salza, a personal friend of Emperor Frederick II, conquered most of the Prussian territories that Conrad had promised him and in whose possession the Knights were confirmed by both the Emperor and the Pope. With the establishment of this new colonial empire in Prussia—and the loss, meantime, of much of Pomerania—Poland was in danger of losing her free access to the Baltic Sea. From now until well into the fifteenth century the quickly Germanized region, administered by a highly dynamic, half ecclesiastical, half military ruling caste, was to be a source of frequent trouble to Poland.

Poland's weakness acted as a challenge to revive the idea of a great West Slav Empire, now under Czech leadership. Young King Wenceslas II, claiming older treaties of inheritance with Piast princes relating to Silesia and Little Poland, occupied Cracow, the Polish capital, early in 1291. His move found opposition from Duke Przemysl of Great Poland who, with encouragement from the Holy See, had himself crowned king in 1295, but was murdered a few months later. Eventually Wenceslas gained recognition in most parts of Poland, where especially the cities and part of the clergy supported him. He was himself crowned King of Poland by the Archbishop of Gniezno in 1300. Czech and Polish historians have frequently disagreed about the character of this short-lived personal union. Some of the king's officials, appointed mostly from the Czech high nobility, did little to make their administration popular. Yet some effective steps were taken toward the needed internal unification. Wenceslas died in 1305. His young son and heir, Wenceslas III, who sometime before, at the extinction of the Árpád dynasty, had been elected and crowned also as king of Hungary, resigned this title and tried to safeguard his position in the two West Slav states. But on his way toward Poland, having been king for little over a year, he was murdered at Olomouc by unknown men and for unknown reasons. With him the male line of the ancient house of Přemysl died, at the time probably the oldest of all European dynasties.

Free from the Czech pressure, at least as an effective force, one of the Polish princes, Władysław Łokietek (The Short), Prince of Kuyavia, gained support in many parts of the country, but had to overcome stiff resistance in others, especially in the Cracow region, until he was crowned as King of Poland at Gniezno in 1320. This time the restoration of the royal office was a solid achievement, especially since Władysław could count on the support of the Avignon papacy as well as of Hungary, while the king of Bohemia—John of Luxemburg—still tried to maintain his own claims on the basis of his succession to the Přemyslids. It was far more serious for Władysław that all his attempts to regain eastern Pomerania and the mouth of the Vistula with the port of Gdańsk (Danzig) failed, at a time when the Order of the Teutonic Knights was at the zenith of its power and established its new capital at Marienburg (Malborg) in the newly conquered West Prussia. For a century and a half Poland was cut off from the sea. It was not accidental that at this very moment and through Władysław Łokietek Poland established, for the first time, close bonds with its northeastern neighbors, the Lithuanians, who had formed a strong state under Grand Duke Gedymin, destined to become the ancestor of a great Polish dynasty. Yet, as the Lithuanians were still heathens, Poland's association with them strengthened the chances of the Teutonic Knights to receive support from Germany and from the king of Bohemia, and may also have strengthened the tendency of the many princes and princelings of Silesia to seek close contact with and protection from Bohemia rather than Poland. This was especially true of the largely Germanized cities of Lower Silesia, with Breslau at their head. Between 1327 and 1330, all Silesian princes did homage to King John. From now on, for the next 410 years, Silesia remained an important part of the realm of the Bohemian crown. For Poland this was a painful loss which, like the loss of Polish Pomerania, she did not easily forget or resign herself to. Yet Władysław's reign, for all the grave territorial losses, had its strong positive aspects, as it was then that the dangerous weakness arising from the multiplicity of dukes and duchies was overcome and the basis laid for future greatness. It was to come with Władysław's son and successor, Casimir (Kazimierz) the Great.

His time was, in many aspects, one of the "golden ages" of Poland. It is rather remarkable that this period largely coincided with equally splendid phases of development in Bohemia and in Hungary and that there, too, rulers of unusual strength and effectiveness bore the crown: Charles IV and Louis I (the Great). It would be wrong to ascribe the greatness of the three old kingdoms of East Central Europe during this period merely to the achievements of their kings; many other factors were involved. Yet all three had at least the will and the skill to make the fullest use of great opportunities. Their reigns overlap somewhat: Casimir from 1333 to 1370, Louis from 1342 to 1382, and Charles from 1346 to 1378. However, Charles had already ruled Bohemia and Moravia as regent with the title of Margrave of Moravia since 1333, and his influence upon the whole period was all the greater as he obtained, as the first of Bohemia's kings, also the crown of the Holy Roman Empire.

Emperor Charles IV

Charles himself was the grandson of Emperor Henry VII, who had married his son John to Elizabeth of Bohemia, the Přemyslid princess and sister of Wenceslas III, who had inherited the crown upon her brother's death after some dynastic struggles. John had been largely an absentee ruler, an ambitious and romantic knight for whom foreign wars were the essence of his kingship. He had gained much, especially nearly all of Silesia and most of Upper Lusatia, and for some time even the rule over a number of the cities of northern Italy. But in his enlarged kingdom his own power was weak, and that of the great lords correspondingly strong. They supported his adventures just because they preferred a king who would leave the government of the realm largely in their own greedy hands. When, in 1333, Charles was charged with the regency he put a stop at least to any further growth of baronial power, but in 1346 he accompanied his father in his campaign in support of his French allies in the Hundred Years War, and at the Battle of Crécy King John, already blind since 1340, fell in a fierce hand-to-hand fight.

Charles's role in German history was considerable, and the harsh judgment of his successor Maximilian I that he was "the Holy Empire's arch-stepfather" has long been refuted by modern historiography. But the first part of Maximilian's statement, that he was "Bohemia's father," was certainly justified. Personally he was as "supranational" as only medieval man could be, and especially a medieval Emperor with a mixture of Czech, German, and French in his blood and in his spiritual heritage. He did not lack a strong feeling of responsibility for the maintenance of what was still substantial and worth saving in the great but shaky structure of the Empire, and the famous "Golden Bull" of 1356 in the main achieved this as well as could be expected. Yet it can hardly be denied that his strongest identification was with his Bohemian heritage. This, of course, must not be understood in terms of modern nationalism. Far from thinking of Czech ethnic and cultural values as opposed to German ones, he did all in his power to promote a maximum of cross-fertilization. He made Prague, in many regards, the center not only of the kingdom but of the Empire as well. He made it (though the date preceded his kingship) into the seat of an archbishopric independent from Mainz. In 1348 he made Prague the seat of the first university founded east of the Rhine and north of the Alps, which very soon became an institution of brilliance and world renown. He instructed the princes of the Empire to have their sons learn the Czech language, the use of which was greatly promoted during his reign. By all these acts he gave the Czech nation a status and a dignity equal to those of the greatest nations of Europe. His economic policy supported the development of the cities, as had that of his Přemyslid predecessors, though generally he favored the patrician elements (which were frequently of German origin) over the flourishing craft guilds, whose growth he tried in vain to stop. In Prague itself the Emperor's foundation and settlement of the "New Town" did, in fact, result in a strengthening of the craft guilds and with them of the Czech elements in the capital. In his attempt to unify and codify the law of the Bohemian realm—in the form of the "Maiestas Carolina"—Charles could not overcome the resistance of the baronial caste, yet much of the legislation unifying the country and strengthening the central power of the crown was passed in detail, and the rich income from the country's silver mines contributed to making the ruler less dependent on the good will of the high nobility.

In the cultural field, too, Charles's court (admired by the visiting Petrarch) presents a high point of Bohemian history. He was one of the greatest builders of the Middle Ages. He called some of the leading foreign architects and sculptors to Prague to take part in his program of church building (for example, the beginning of the Cathedral of St. Vitus on the Prague Castle hill). His patronage also helped that great domestic art which, in the times from the middle of the fourteenth to the middle of the fifteenth century, flourished especially in the form of Bohemia's gothic painting.

In his foreign policy Charles achieved extraordinary successes for the house of Luxemburg. Already in the time of his regency he was able, in 1335, to gain recognition from King Casimir of Poland for his possession of Silesia. To his other acquisitions belonged Lower Lusatia and the March of Brandenburg, the latter giving the Luxemburg house a second electoral vote. Brandenburg was passed on, in 1415, to the Hohenzollerns, but Lusatia, where many rural areas were inhabited by Slav people, the Wends or Lusatian Serbs, remained with Bohemia for almost three centuries, until the time of the Thirty Years' War.

In sharp contrast to his father, Charles IV did not really like war, and the greater part of his vast acquisitions was achieved by diplomatic means and dynastic family ties. Long before his death, these tactics had made the house of Luxemburg the greatest power in Europe, yet he hoped for more. His own family—including two brothers, three sons, and three nephews—seemed sure of survival for generations to come, but the king of Poland, Casimir, was the only one of his line and had only daughters, and Louis of Hungary was in a similar position. It seemed a challenge for Charles to win for his house the succession in both the other kingdoms of East Central Europe. He was partly successful. While he was not able to obtain a change in the solemn treaties promising Louis the succession in Poland if Casimir died without male heir, he did obtain the hand of Louis' daughter Mary for his younger son Sigismund, who subsequently succeeded as king of Hungary upon Louis' death in 1382. His first born, Wenceslas, was, even before Charles's death, crowned King of Bohemia and elected King of the Romans, but he was not the man to continue the work of his brilliant father.

Casimir III of Poland

In many ways Casimir III could be compared to Charles IV. Like the Luxemburg ruler, the last in the reigning line of the Piasts was, on the whole, a man of peace who tried, wherever possible, to strengthen his country by diplomatic rather than military means. As

Charles did, he established a strong central government by at least partial taming of the great feudal lords. As Charles (and his Přemyslid predecessors) did, he favored the cities which, at this time, had not yet developed in Poland as strongly as those in Bohemia and Moravia. He, too, tried, with only partial success, to unify and codify his country's law, and he, too, was a great builder. In some fields it is obvious that Casimir consciously followed the example of his powerful neighbor; in 1364, he established a university in Cracow which, however, did not reach the fame and the power of attraction of the older school until in the fifteenth century, as a consequence of the Hussite revolution, the University of Prague became, as it seemed, the training ground of heretics. Casimir did more than Charles for the peasants of his country. He also was an especially benevolent protector of the Jews who, in this time, immigrated in large numbers to Poland from the West, where they had been persecuted as being responsible for the "Black Death."

The relationship between the two great rulers was somewhat ambivalent, and remained so until Casimir's death in 1370, though it seems obvious that they respected one another and that both generally tried to avoid an open collision. Casimir, clearly, was reluctant to abandon Silesia, yet he did this because in return he obtained the renunciation by the king of Bohemia of earlier claims to Polish kingship. By gaining security in relation to his southern and western neighbors (it was equally important to make sure that the Teutonic Knights would receive no further help or encouragement from Prague) he could move more freely eastward, where there were opportunities for expansion on the basis of hereditary claims. Above all, Casimir gained Galicia with the city of Lwów (Lemberg), as well as parts of Volhynia, for which he had to wage a war with Lithuania. His policy toward this great and still expanding realm—the only sizable part of Europe that had not accepted Christianity—was, however, not one of enmity but rather one directed toward better understanding, which seemed doubly important in view of the strength of Poland's and Lithuania's common enemy, the Teutonic Knights. The idea of a close Polish-Lithuanian relationship, based naturally upon prior acceptance of the Roman creed by the Lithuanian ducal family and nobility, began to be considered in Poland at this time. But it could only be realized 16 years after Casimir's death.

At that moment Louis of Hungary, in agreement with the treaties concluded between the two kings, became Poland's king as well. But to Poland this personal union did more harm than good. Louis, on the whole, was an absentee ruler, treating Poland more or less like an annex to Hungary. Also, in order to minimize Polish resistance to his rule, he granted a charter in 1374, at the town of Košice in Northern Hungary (Eastern Slovakia), which, among other guarantees, almost completely freed the Polish nobility from paying any taxes to the king. This was the first act in a long line of royal concessions to the Polish Estates, some of which were destined in later centuries to condemn the crown to progressive impotence

Lithuania and the Teutonic Knights

After Louis' death in 1382 (and an interregnum filled with much confusion) his daughter Jadwiga (Hedwig) was elected reigning queen, and two years later she was married to the grand duke of Lithuania, Jagiello, who, upon receiving baptism together with his relatives and most of his nobility, called himself forthwith Władysław and was crowned king as Jadwiga's co-ruler. The marriage was a historical event of the greatest significance as it tied together, for centuries to come, the fate of the Kingdom of Poland with that of the less highly civilized but far more extended Grand Duchy of Lithuania which, beside Lithuanians, contained large numbers of Byelorussians and Ukrainians (Ruthenians). The personal union between the two territories did not immediately result in a full coordination of policy between them. Indeed, Władysław, officially still the head of both nations, was in danger of losing all influence in Lithuania when his gifted and ambitious cousin Witold gained, for a time, the support of the Teutonic Knights in his attempt to establish himself as the independent ruler of Lithuania. Finally, in 1392, Władysław granted to his cousin the position of grand duke of Lithuania as long as he recognized the king of Poland as his liege lord, an arrangement that from now on permitted close cooperation of the royal cousins; the arrangement was confirmed in 1400 by a special, permanent treaty of alliance approved by the nobility of both countries and clearly directed against the one enemy that seemed to threaten them both most seriously—the Prussian Order of the Teutonic Knights.

Lithuania's conversion to Christianity deprived the Order of its usual pretext for further eastward expansion. But struggle between the Polish-Lithuanian alliance and the Knights was not allayed. It broke out in 1409, essentially over the issue of Samogitia, an old province of Lithuania and its only exit to the Baltic Sea, which the Prussian Knights had desired and occupied as the land bridge between their own territories and those of the closely related Livonian Knights of the Sword. In July 1410 the combined Polish-Lithuanian army—supported also by some troops hired in Bohemia—gained an overwhelming victory over the Order in the battle of Grünwald (Tannenberg), which seemed to decide the war in one stroke. The resistance of the Order proved more stubborn and prolonged than had been anticipated, and the peace concluded at Toruń (Thorn) in 1411, while forcing the Knights to leave Samogitia, for the time being, in the hands of Lithuania, gave little to Poland. Nonetheless, the myth of invincibility that had surrounded the Knights was destroyed and they were henceforth on the defensive against the growing strength of the Polish-Lithuanian federation.

In the minds of many people, not only in Poland but also in Bohemia, this was a great blow delivered by Slavic men and arms to German expansionist greed. The traditionally friendly attitude of the Czech kings toward the Order had been much weakened under Wenceslas IV; he had not objected to the leading role which one of his prominent courtiers (Nicholas Sokol of Lamberg) had played in leading Czech troops to help the Poles in 1410, and among the letters that King Władysław received after his great victory of Grünwald was one written by a master and professor at the University of Prague. His name was Jan Hus.

THREE

The Age of the Czech Reformation

The Hussite Age is, in the historical consciousness of the Czech people, of an importance to which nothing else in its history can be compared. This is fully justified. Not only was it the most heroic age of this small nation but it was also the time when its influence on, and contributions to, European political, social, religious, and cultural developments were especially significant.

The roots of the movement go back into the fourteenth century. It had much to do with the extraordinary economic and political power the church had acquired, which was, especially in the form of landed wealth, probably larger in Bohemia and Moravia than in most other European countries. The resentment which was thereby caused in wide circles of the population was not only directed against the domestic church organization; there was also increasing indignation directed against Rome, where Bohemia was long considered (and treated) as an especially welcome source of income.

There existed, at the same time, the beginning of an important reform movement within the church in Bohemia. One of the earliest great reform preachers was an Augustinian from Austria, Conrad Waldhauser, whom Charles IV called to Prague about 1360 and who began attacking simony and moral decay, especially in the clergy. Still more effective and vigorous in his criticism was Milíč of Kroměříž (Kremsier), a Czech friend of Waldhauser's and Prague archdeacon, who would probably have become a victim of the Inquisition had it not been for the protection of Charles IV. The greatest of Hus's predecessors was the Czech theologian Matthias of Janov. In his attack upon a corrupt clergy he presented thoughts which, with their biblicism and their emphasis on true piety as far superior to all priestly ministrations, began the approach toward a Protestant mentality that was also to characterize his great disciple Jan Hus.

Thus, the tradition of a Czech reform movement was already strong when about 1400 the spread of John Wyclif's thoughts in Bohemia became a burning issue between the reforming wing of the masters of Prague University and the high clergy. Wyclif's works had, by this time, found wide circulation in various regions of Central Europe and especially at the University of Prague, partly through earlier contacts between Prague and Oxford. Much of his thought, revolutionary in religious and philosophical terms and at least considered revolutionary in other ways by all those interested in maintaining the social structure, was accepted by Hus and his friends simply because so much of it corresponded to their own ideas and was strikingly formulated. For the same reasons Wyclif's teachings became the object of energetic attacks on the part of the church, including even groups which could be identified as reformist, such as, for example, the Gallicanist wing of the French high clergy, led by Jean Gerson. Indeed, the cautious reformers could be expected to be even more implacable in their antagonism to the more revolutionary wing as they had to prove that in terms of dogma there was, in their case, not even the shadow of a suspicion of heretical leanings.

Thus it came about that Jan Hus, the Prague master and professor who had stood up against clerical power and wealth, against papal absolutism and simony, and against the sale of indulgences, found himself cited, with a promise of safe conduct from King Sigismund, before the great Council of Constance, the first of the two ecumenical councils that together formed the high point of the conciliar movement of the fourteenth and fifteenth centuries.

The council was presided over by Sigismund, the younger son of Charles IV who had, since 1387, been king of Hungary and was elected King of the Romans in 1410. At that date he had, as head of the Empire, finally replaced his older brother Wenceslas IV who had, already in 1400, been deposed as King of the Romans by a majority of the electors. During the earlier years of Wenceslas' reign much of the great achievements of his father, not only in the Empire but also in Bohemia, had been lost. While not quite the ever-drunken monster he has sometimes been described as, Wenceslas was far from a competent ruler, and the power of the crown had become seriously weakened, to the extent that twice during his reign he was held as a prisoner for several months, first by a clique of lords, which only freed him after he had been blackmailed into making considerable concessions to the baronial caste, then by his brother Sigismund, king of Hungary, who thereby hoped to gain a firm position in Bohemia as well. Wenceslas, however, was popular with the urban population, especially in Prague, and his policy in relation to the reformatory tendencies in Prague was generally favorable. Of special significance was his decision, in 1408, to support conciliarism and the calling of a church council in Pisa as against the unconditional backing of Pope Gregory XII. The issue came before the University of Prague. When three out of its four "nations" (the Bavarian, Saxon, and Polish) decided against the king, he issued, in 1409, the Decree of Kutná Hora, which gave the Bohemian "nation" 3 votes against one only for the other 3 "nations." The decision led to a mass exodus of German teachers and students (many of whom went to found a university in Leipzig) and changed the character of the University of Prague into that of a more narrowly national institution in which, furthermore, the new reform movement soon found a strong spiritual and intellectual center. Prague's isolation, in turn, helped the University of Cracow, which had, after a period of stagnation, started on a new, more prosperous phase at the beginning of the fifteenth century.

After the German exodus, Hus was appointed rector of the university, but was soon afterward, under Catholic pressure, forced to leave Prague for southern Bohemia. Preaching under open skies he contributed to the early growth of a movement of peasants and other "little people" which later crystallized into Taboritism.

The situation in Bohemia had then, in the first half of the second decade of the fifteenth century, become full of tensions, of which the religious antagonism was the most openly expressed. But at the back of it there was also the resentment of the middle and lower classes in the cities against the patricians—mostly German—and of the peasants against their landlords, ecclesiastical as well as temporal. The time became ripe for a revolution.

But it was the religious issue, combined with national feelings, that directly led to the explosion. The first in this chain of events was the decision of the Council of Constance to burn Jan Hus as a heretic. Hus had been so popular a figure in the Czech lands that his execution was considered a terrible insult by almost the whole Czech nation, including the great majority of its nobility. Yet it took four more years until the attempt of King Wenceslas' government to take Prague churches out of the hands of the reformers led, in July 1419, to the open outbreak of insurrection in the capital. Hopes to contain this explosion disappeared when, immediately afterwards, King Wenceslas died and his brother Sigismund demanded the right to succeed him. The great majority of the Czech people who now adhered to the reform regarded the last of the Luxemburgs as fully responsible for the death of the martyr of Constance, and were determined not to let him become their king. But Sigismund himself was just as determined to take what he had long considered his rightful heritage, all the more as he was constantly short of money and the income from the rich Bohemian silver mines appeared to him as much the easiest way to solve this problem. It seemed convenient that he could now present, to the church and the Empire, his campaign for the subjection of the rebellious Czechs as a crusade against criminal heretics.

On their part, the Czechs were far from united, even from the beginning. Part of the high nobility and, to a lesser extent, some of the well-to-do members of the patriciate of Prague and other cities would have preferred to come to terms with Sigismund, whereas the more radical elements did not even want to consider his acceptance and a middle group, led by some masters of the university, tried to maintain a compromise position. These various groups finally, in late spring of 1420, accepted, as a sort of national charter, the Four Articles of Prague, demanding (1) the free preaching of the Word of God; (2) the dispensing of both elements of the Eucharist, bread and wine, to laymen; (3) the abolition of power and wealth wielded by priests, who should be led back to apostolic poverty; and (4) the proper punishment of all mortal sins, especially those committed publicly.

Of these articles, the one of the greatest importance was the demand for the communion in both kinds (*sub utraque specie*; hence the term "Utraquist" for the adherents of this ritual). The man who had introduced this change, actually a return to older forms, was Hus's friend, Jacobellus of Stříbro (Mies), one of the leading theologians of the University of Prague. Its significance was much greater than appears at first sight: it implied an attack upon the claim to a special position of the clergy as belonging to a higher order of humans, and a change of the priestly function to that of ministership.

The chalice, in the further course of the movement, became the symbol of the Hussite movement, it appeared on all Hussite banners and was chosen by Jan Zižka, the greatest, most dynamic figure of the revolution, as the name of his castle and his family.

Zižka came from an impoverished clan of squires of southern Bohemia, was for a while a leader of mercenaries, took part in the Polish campaign of 1410 against the Teutonic Knights and later rose in King Wenceslas' service to the rank of captain of the palace guard. Yet he took part in the first uprising of July 1419, and before long became the organizer and military leader of the armies of the radical groups, consisting mostly of peasants and townsmen of southern Bohemia and centered in the newly founded fortress-town of Tábor.

The Taborite movement attempted to establish a pure theocracy. Its religious ideas were strongly influenced by radical biblicism, harsh puritanism expressed in iconoclastic destruction of monasteries and images, and above all by chiliastic expectations that encouraged the belief that the coming kingdom of Christ would eliminate all inequalities. This belief led, in the early phases of the revolution, to a measure of economic communism which, however, was soon abandoned. In one of the most radical developments within the Taborite community, that of the Adamites (influenced by the earlier movement in Picardy, Flanders, and western Germany, of the Brethren of the Free Spirit) a wild anarchism was coupled with the advocacy of sexual licence, but this group was largely exterminated as it collided with the severe puritanism that characterized the Taborite brotherhood as a whole. The Taborites remained the most determined representatives of a policy of noncompromise with Rome, expressed also by the daring step to dispense with apostolic succession and instead to elect their own bishop. Taborite troops, led by Žižka, participated in the defense of Prague against the first great "crusade" led by Sigismund against the heretics, and in July 1420 defeated the far larger royalist army at the Battle of the Vítkov. More decisive, in the long run, was Žižka's ability to create formidable armies out of peasant levies. They were equipped with flails, crossbows, and guns, and were organized in well disciplined tactical units whose main elements were large horse-drawn battle wagons. These could, in remarkably swift moves, be put in position, mostly on hills, as movable fortresses which the feudal cavalry of the enemy attacked in vain. Eventually Žižka used fire weapons, for the first time in history, as actual field artillery. They contributed notably to his decisive victories over Sigismund when the latter invaded the Kingdom of Bohemia in the winter of 1421-22 with a large, mostly Hungarian army.

Even before this important campaign the Hussites had attempted, with some success, to unite the nation by summoning to Čáslav a meeting of the Estates of the whole realm in which representatives of Bohemia and Moravia participated. This great diet was officially called by the city council of Prague, which for the time being had functioned as a national government. The assembly solemnly deposed Sigismund, agreed to offer the crown to the King of Poland, and meantime appointed a regency council of twenty men, half of them representing the cities (among them four from Prague, two from Tábor), one quarter the lords, the other quarter the knights and squires. The unity thus temporarily achieved, largely under the lead of Prague, did not last. In Prague itself there were severe struggles between some of the influential masters of the university, who favored a generally more conservative attitude, and a far more revolutionary group led by the brilliant and popular Jan Želivský, originally a Premonstratensian monk who soon became the undisputed leader of the economically lower groups, especially many members of the craft guilds and the workers and day-laborers without guild standing as well. Želivský had closely cooperated with Tábor, and for a while he seemed the most powerful man in all Bohemia, but in March 1422 a conspiracy of his enemies in the baronial camp and among the Prague citizenry led to the capture and execution of Želivský and of many of his leading disciples. It was the first attempt made by the conservative element to arrest the course of the revolutionary movement and to undo many of its achievements. This attempt at an early reversal preceded the arrival, in Bohemia, of the Lithuanian prince, Sigismund Korybut, a nephew of King Władysław of Poland and of his cousin Witold. After Władysław had refused the Bohemian crown Witold had, with reservations, accepted it. He had told the Pope that he was taking the Czechs under his protection so as to facilitate the needed reconciliation of this nation with Rome. Witold's decision, and Władysław's somewhat reluctant agreement with it, was based on the hope that thereby Sigismund could be weakened and prevented from further supporting the Teutonic Knights. Korybut, in Bohemia, proclaimed himself viceroy for Witold as the elected king, and was accepted by the majority of the Hussite groups including, after some difficulties, also Žižka and his Taborites. But, after little more than a year, during which the Polish-Lithuanian support seemed to add much strength to Hussite Bohemia, Korybut was recalled and the Czechs were as isolated as before.

During the year 1422 Žižka got into a serious conflict with the leading Taborite priests who had adopted an understanding of the Eucharist that denied transubstantiation and anticipated much of the later Eucharistic theology of Zwingli. Žižka left Tábor and took over the leadership of the eastern Bohemian brotherhood of the Orebites with the center at Hradec Králové (Königgrätz). With a position that was religiously and politically somewhat left of center he gained, partly by political and partly by military means, the adherence of an increasingly strong coalition of cities many of which had previously been under the leadership of Prague or of Tábor. This struggle developed into a full-scale civil war when the Prague patricians, having regained the leadership in the city, allied themselves with a baronial coalition, which included even some of the leading Catholic royalists. This war was decided by a brilliant victory that Žižka gained, in June 1424, at Malešov over the conservative coalition. In the following months national unity, under Žižka's leadership, was reestablished to the extent that he could lead an army of all Hussite groups—Orebites, Taborites, and Praguers—in a campaign destined to free Moravia from the encroachments of Duke Albert of Austria, Sigismund's son-in-law and heir. But on this campaign Žižka became a victim of the plague.

The paramount position that had been attained in Bohemia by the two brotherhoods and city leagues of the Taborites and Orebites under Žižka's leadership (the Orebites were called "Orphans" after his death), survived for another decade. In this period they clearly dominated the domestic scene, while the role of the high nobility—with individual exceptions—remained limited. Prague, too, was much weakened after an attempt of Prince Korybut to gain the Czech crown for himself had failed, and was the scene of repeated collisions between the more conservative elements in the Old Town and the craft guilds in the New Town who were trying to ally with the Orphans. But the most important change of these years, mainly from

1428 to 1433, was the fact that the Czechs now no longer waited for the enemies to launch crusades into Bohemia but finally decided to attack them in their own territory in order to make them more ready to think of peace. The man who first conceived of this change toward an offensive strategy and who, after Žižka, was the most brilliant leader of the "Warriors of God," was a Taborite priest-general, Prokop the Bald or the Great (as he was called to distinguish him from his friend, Prokop the Lesser or the Short, who commanded the Orphans). Those offensive thrusts were directed, at various times, toward Austria, Hungary, and various parts of Germany; the Czechs called them "spanile jízdy" ("noble" or "beauteous rides") but the victims considered them as horrifying invasions which could not be stopped or defeated except by buying off the invaders with considerable payments of money and goods. One of the most remarkable attacks arose out of a renewal of the alliance between the Czechs and Poland. In 1433 a strong Hussite army, mostly Orphans, marched through Greater Poland into the Western territories of the Teutonic Knights, conquered the important town of Tczew (Dirschau) and contributed much to the decision of the Prussian Grand Master to sue for peace. In their reports home the Czechs could say that nothing barred their victorious march north until they reached the shores of the Baltic Sea.

As all the later "crusades," undertaken in 1426, 1427, and 1431, ended in utter disaster while the Czech offensive actions were almost without exception successful, the Church of Rome as well as the Emperor Sigismund began to think of the possible conclusion of peace. Preliminary negotiations conducted at Cheb in 1431 and 1432 led finally to an invitation of the Czechs to send a delegation to the great Council of Basel. A Czech delegation, with Prokop the Great and the Prague Master John Rokycana in the lead, was received in Basel with all honors—a remarkable change from the way in which Jan Hus had been treated. After difficult negotiations, at times interrupted for lengthy periods, some sort of agreement seemed to be within view. But before it could be consummated a last great conflict arose between the Czech parties. As had happened ten years earlier, the majority of the nobility allied itself with the government of the Old Town of Prague, and one of the first steps was the occupation, by conservative forces, of the New Town, which had still been allied with the city leagues of the two brotherhoods. On May 30, 1434, a full-scale battle fought at Lipany between the field armies of the brotherhoods and the conservative coalition reversed the earlier decision of Malešov and destroyed much, though by no means all, of the military power of the Taborites and Orphans, whose leaders, the two Prokops, both fell. It was an effective "Thermidor," essentially ending the period of the supremacy of the brotherhoods and town leagues over the nobility. Yet the great blow did not reestablish the situation as it had existed before the revolution. While the great barons returned into a leading position, the church had lost and did not regain the major part of its gigantic landed wealth and power. The baronial strength was partly balanced by a much stronger economic and political position of the knights and squires, and even the strength of the towns, though reduced by the blow of Lipany, was superior to what it had been before 1419.

In consequence the hope of some circles at the Council of Basel that the Czechs would bow to the demand for complete conformity was soon shown to be an illusion. The outcome of the negotiations rested essentially on the basis that had already been established before Lipany. It took the form of the Compactata (Basel Compacts), which, in July 1436, were pronounced and solemnly confirmed by the Emperor Sigismund in the Moravian city of Jihlava. Sigismund was finally recognized as king of Bohemia and took his residence in Prague, but the last of the Luxemburgs died in the following year and was succeeded, not without considerable difficulties, by his son-in-law, the Habsburg Albert II. He and his successors had to confirm, and to promise to protect, the Basel Compacts.

The Compacts were, essentially, a somewhat watered-down version of the Four Articles of Prague. What seemed most important, at least to the Czechs, was the concession that the chalice was to be given to laymen in Bohemia and Moravia who requested it and had "had this custom." They did not foresee that this reference to the custom could eventually be understood in personal terms. Without this concession, in any case, the Czech negotiators, led during the last phase by the Utraquist priest and master John Rokycana, would never have accepted the rest of the peace arrangements, including Sigismund's recognition.

The Compacts, indeed, were to gain extraordinary significance in the history of the following decades. They were never officially confirmed by the Holy See, though the Czechs, throughout a quarter of a century, again and again petitioned the Popes for just this. The Compacts did, as it were, become a cornerstone of "peaceful coexistence" between the Hussites, mainly represented by the Utraquist church, and the Catholics. It was remarkable enough that for the greater part of the next 30 years Catholic and Hussite-Utraquist could and did live beside each other, not always in peace and friendship—as yet each hoped either to convince and convert or eventually overcome the other—but at least without slaughtering one another. But a real, solid stabilization of internal conditions and full domestic peace was not gained until the young heir of a baronial family with strong Hussite traditions, George of Poděbrady, gained in rapid sequence first (in 1448) the leadership of Czech Utraquism and the possession of the city of Prague, then (in 1452) the regency, ruling the country for Sigismund's grandson, the boy-king Ladislav Posthumus, and finally (in 1458), upon the king's premature death of the plague, the crown itself. During the two decades of his rule (he died in 1471) Bohemia entered the short but remarkable age of a strong constitutional kingship which seemed to give hope for a development not unlike that of Tudor England or Vasa Sweden. King George managed, throughout the greater part of his reign, to reestablish the position of the crown in a way which would limit the influence and destroy the dominance of the baronial class, partly by restoring a judicial system less onesidedly relying on the barons, partly by giving positions of influence to members of the gentry and of the upper classes of the cities, especially Prague. Economically, politically, and in her international position Bohemia recovered to an astonishing degree under King George. His strong policy led, however, to a slowly growing resistance among some of the leading barons who eventually decided to use the religious issue for maneuvers intended to undermine George's position. This was made much easier for them by the policy of the papacy.

Pope Pius II, the former Cardinal Enea Silvio de'Piccolomini, had established a very friendly relationship with George of Poděbrady even prior to his accession to the throne and had also helped him in his endeavor to gain international recognition. But he had done this in the hope that George, in return, would eliminate all forms of deviation from Catholic rites, above all the chalice for the laity. He did not really understand the significance the chalice, and the Compacts that protected it, had gained for the majority of the Czech people, and overrated not only the king's willingness but also his ability to suppress Hussitism and Utraquism in Bohemia and Moravia. A proper mixture of friendliness and pressure, the Pope thought, would get the desired action going, especially since George had sworn at his coronation a secret and somewhat ambiguous oath that he would suppress all heresy in the country. When, in 1462, a solemn embassy carrying George's message of "obedience" asked for final confirmation of the Compacts, the Pope, believing that George was playing an insincere political game, declared the Compacts invalid and demanded immediate cessation of all Hussite services as well as other measures insuring complete conformity with the Roman ritual. George answered that he had stood and would stand by the Compacts, which he felt the Pope had no right to revoke and without which there could be no peace in the Czech realm. At first the greater part of the Catholics in Bohemia, including not only the Czechs but also the Germans in Bohemia's border regions and in the larger cities of Moravia, supported the king, fearing that an open outbreak of the religious struggle would destroy the precious peace that George had established after the long times of civil war and chaos. George, in spite of the activities of the Curia, was even able for a while to improve his international position, especially by strengthening ties with Poland and France. One of the most interesting (and in terms of the history of political thought, most important) forms in which King George sought to counter the attack of the papacy was the launching of a plan for an international league of princes for the maintenance of peace in Europe. This should enable the Christian world to withstand the steadily growing threat from the Ottoman Turks, but for the sake of peace it should persist even without regard to this special menace. For the first time in history this plan put all the burden for the maintenance of international peace upon an organization of the sovereign lay states, dropping all references to the old and obsolete notion of a Christian commonwealth held together and directed by Emperor and Pope. From the institution of the great councils, especially that of Constance, the plan borrowed the organization of the membership in "nationes," in fact regions, which served to develop careful if complex voting procedures. Beside a council representing the members there would be an international law court to decide on all disagreements between members who would, upon entrance, solemnly renounce all use of war against other members. The organization would have its own treasury, its own coins, its own military force and power of international taxation. The central offices of the organization would shift every 5 years from one region to another, beginning in Basel. The whole plan was worked out and diplomatic steps were taken for it, after careful consultation with and complete agreement with King Casimir of Poland. The presidency of the organization was, in 1464, offered by a Czech embassy to King Louis XI of France who, however, was reluctant to take sides too openly against the papacy. It is easy to see today that a political concept so far advanced beyond its time could not succeed. It is still remarkable that it could be conceived of at all—a worthy predecessor to Sully's "Grand Design" and to Wilson's League.

What remained in substance of George's diplomacy was the general alliance with France and, more important, with Poland. King Casimir was, in the following years, repeatedly encouraged, even implored, by George's enemies to join them and lead them against the "heretics" and in return receive the Pope's blessing for taking the crown of St. Wenceslas, to which, as a son-in-law of King Albert II, he felt he had a claim. He had, however, good reason to decline, especially in view of his long war with the Prussian Knights, and his own answer was that "he did not think that a crowned and anointed king could thus be deposed." The wish of the papacy to have a strong ruler act as executor of its sentence against Hussite Bohemia was finally fulfilled by King George's erstwhile son-in-law, Matthias Hunyadi, called Corvinus, the young king of Hungary.

By the time that Matthias invaded Moravia the Czech kingdom had already passed through more than a year of civil war resulting from an open rebellion of part of the high nobility, which was supported by the papal excommunication of the king. But until the beginning of 1468 the military situation of the rebels had steadily deteriorated. It was only Matthias' interference that made the "second Hussite War" into a life-and-death struggle in which the very survival not only of George's kingship but also of the Czech national reformation was at stake. During the second half of 1468 Matthias, in alliance with the rebellious barons as well as with Emperor Frederick III, was largely successful and managed to occupy the greater part of Moravia. But in the following year, attempting to invade Bohemia too, Matthias and his army were completely surrounded; he tried to buy his way out of this dangerous situation by agreeing to conclude an armistice and promising to intercede with Rome for peace with Bohemia. Instead he used the time thus gained to put pressure on his baronial allies who, in May 1469, in the Moravian city of Olomouc, elected him king of Bohemia. Yet the war now went generally in favor of George, to the extent that early in 1471 most of his enemies, not only many of the Czech Catholic barons and the Emperor but even Pope Paul II, were ready for a compromise peace, acknowledging again George's kingship and the limited right of the Czechs to have the Holy Communion in the "two kinds." Just in the moment of impending victory George, not quite 51 years old, died of an illness on March 22, 1471. With him ended the second phase of the Hussite age; with him also died the hope for a strong constitutional monarchy in the Bohemian realm. Under his successor, Vladislav II, oldest son of Casimir Jagiello of Poland-Lithuania, the baronial caste was to regain all it had lost in the preceding years, and Bohemia became a "Ständestaat" (state dominated by the Estates). But for more than half a century the two West Slav realms were now closely tied together under one dynasty, the house of Jagiello.

In 1490, at the death of Matthias Corvinus, King Vladislav of Bohemia was also elected king of Hungary, and from then on the realms of Bohemia and Hungary, under a full personal union, were brought together even more closely than Bohemia and Poland. This union had also some consequences for the development of the Slovaks, and for the Czech-Slovak relationship.

To some extent a Czech impact on northern Hungary, the land of the Slovaks, can be noted even before 1490. During the later phases of the Hussite revolution, Czech partisans and soldiers had gone east, and a good many of them served under a gifted Czech nobleman, Jan Jiskra of Brandýs who had become a protagonist of Hapsburg interests in Hungary. There, for many years, he dominated with his Czech soldiers most of the Slovak regions, and while he himself was not—at least not during the time of his Hungarian activities—a Hussite, most of his soldiers were. To what extent such Hussite leanings influenced the Slovak population is an issue strongly debated and difficult to judge. While in Bohemia a great majority of the towns were Hussite, the towns in upper Hungary were rather opposed to the Czech partisans, whom they frequently considered and feared as lawless robbers. The leading social groups in those cities were at this time still predominantly German in origin and language. However, quite a few of the Slovak-speaking gentry of those parts seem to have been attracted by Hussite ideas. There were many partisans in the country after Jiskra's armies had been disbanded including Slovak peasants who had lost their homes through war. King Matthias hired some of those partisans, and his best troops, the so-called "Black Legion," consisted largely of Czech mercenaries; on the other hand, Matthias destroyed all those partisan troops that tried to fight independently.

That there was a Czech cultural influence in upper Hungary at this time (even though its Hussite character may be under dispute) can be seen from the fact that the Czech language, as the written language most closely corresponding to spoken Slovak, was used to an increasing extent in Slovakia and by other governments, including the chancery of King Matthias and of his Jagellon successors in Buda, for correspondence not only with Bohemia but also with Slovak noblemen and with some Slovak towns.

It would probably be wrong to conclude from this anything more than the existence of the beginnings of a rather vague feeling of kinship between the great majority of the Slovaks (who as yet hardly conceived of the idea of nationhood) and the politically far more highly developed Czechs. Two things occurred, however, during the early sixteenth century that helped to bring about the first elements of a consciousness of the Slovak people—mostly led by the Slovak-speaking gentry—that they were a group separate from the Magyars and from other ethnic groups within Hungary. One was the invasion of Hungary by the Turks, with the consequence that for a long time there were three Hungaries: a central part completely under Turkish rule; an eastern, Transylvanian part, tributary to the Sultan but in fact independent and ruled by Transylvanian princes of Magyar origin; and finally a northwestern section, the only one where the election of a Hapsburg (Ferdinand I) by the Hungarian estates became effective. In this early Hapsburg-Hungary, therefore, the Slovak element was far stronger in proportion to the total of the population than it had ever been before.

The other factor which helped in leading to the awakening of Slovak consciousness was the coming of the Reformation. It entered Hungary in the two forms of Lutheranism and Calvinism, but while the latter was especially influential among Magyars and in Transylvania, the Slovaks were much more attracted by Lutheranism. Eventually, it is true, the Counter Reformation, vigorously backed by the Hapsburgs everywhere, regained the adherence to Rome of a majority of the Slovak people. Yet among the Slovak gentry and intelligentsia Lutheranism maintained a foothold, and its adherents remained one of the most active, culturally productive and nationally conscious elements of the Slovak people in the period down to the later eighteenth century.

FOUR

The Jagiellons

The victory at Grünwald in 1410 was the high point in the earlier part of Władysław Jagiello's reign. It had been achieved through close cooperation of the two cousins—Jagiello and Witold—who, in their early years, had been repeatedly in severe conflict. It was of greater importance that the bond between Poland and Lithuania, at first based purely on the uncertain personal relationship between the two rulers, was almost immediately after the end of the Prussian war put on a more substantial basis. A treaty concluded in 1413 at Horodło by the princes and representatives of the nobility of both nations tried to stabilize the relationship between them. It was determined that, under the suzerainty of the king of Poland, Lithuania would continue to have her own grand duke even after Witold's death. While this underlined Lithuania's separate position, another measure made the union closer than it had been before. The Polish high nobility, represented at this time by 47 clans, adopted as relatives an equal number of Lithuanian and Ruthenian boyars, with each family sharing the coat-of-arms of the adopting Polish clan. The measure was of considerable significance as a substantial bridge between the leading social groups of the two countries. It was also the beginning of a process of Polonization, and we eventually find several families of Lithuanian and Ruthenian origin playing leading roles in the history of Poland.

The Hussite revolution confronted King Władysław and Grand Duke Witold with difficult problems. They were understandably reluctant to support a movement that was, in Rome and elsewhere, considered to be heretical, especially since it might revive the claim of the Prussian Order that fighting the Lithuanians was meritorious. But, since the Roman Emperor, King Sigismund of Hungary, supported the Knights wherever he could, the two cousins, and especially Witold, took for limited periods the side of the Czech rebellion. On the other hand, Władysław feared that Poland might become infected by the heretical "poison," and strong measures were considered necessary to stem its spread in Poland. Several groups in Poland were attracted by the great reform movement, notably in Great Poland and among members of the lower nobility. Even among the king's advisers the Czechs had friends, and they supported the policy of temporary cooperation with Hussite Bohemia. On the other side a gifted young prelate, Zbigniew Oleśnicki, King Władysław's personal secretary and adviser who became bishop of Cracow and was later Poland's first cardinal, fought with all his strength against this cooperation. His influence became especially strong after King Władysław's death in 1434. His successor, Władysław III, the older son of his fourth, late marriage, was in 1440 elected king of Hungary by the anti-Hapsburg party led mainly by John Hunyadi, famous as a victorious fighter against the Turks. In 1443 Hunyadi and the young king of Poland and Hungary went on a common crusade into the Turkish-occupied northern Balkan regions. Overconfident after several early successes, they tried to attack the Ottoman capital Adrianople but were soon isolated near Varna, where in 1444 their army was destroyed and the king fell in the battle. Polish interest in further anti-Turkish crusades was thereby considerably impaired.

Only three years later Władysław's brother Casimir, since 1440 grand duke of Lithuania, was elected king of Poland, and he soon made sure that in all legal matters Lithuania's equality was maintained without giving her a separate ruler. From now on the king of Poland—except for two very short periods after 1492 and 1544—was to be also the grand duke of Lithuania, thus establishing the strong tradition of personal union. Casimir also succeeded in settling the old struggle between his two realms over Podolia and Volhynia, the first one going to Poland, the second to Lithuania. Casimir IV, a cautious, patient yet fairly strong ruler, was generally averse to any risky adventures and thus made no attempts either to expand his power to the southeast (though he maintained Polish claims to the suzerainty over Moldavia) nor to the southwest where, being married to a daughter of Albert, former Emperor and king of Bohemia, he had certain claims to the crown of St. Wenceslas. Instead he looked north toward the territories of the Teutonic Knights, part of which, notably Eastern Pomerania including Danzig, had been gained by the Prussian Order only in the early fourteenth century, thereby cutting Poland off from the Baltic Sea. The opportunity for a decisive step arose when the German cities and many members of the gentry in the Prussian lands rebelled against the oppressive rule of the Order, joined up in a defense league, and put themselves under the protection of the Polish king. Casimir accepted the offer of the rebelling league and undertook an offensive against the Knights. He had expected a short war and an easy victory, but in this he was mistaken. Supported by the king of Denmark and some German princes, the Teutonic Knights proved to be still strong and dangerous enemies. The war against them was costly and lasted 13 years.

In this war Czech troops, hired by Casimir, played a not inconsiderable role. Also the fact that Casimir was engaged in it for so long was at least a contributing factor in his policy of friendship with King George of Bohemia. At the same time he never gave up the hope that Bohemia would eventually accept a member of the Jagiellon dynasty as king.

While as a military enterprise the long Prussian war brought less glory to Polish arms than the war of 1409-11, the outcome, called the second Peace of Toruń (1466), was far more profitable for Poland. All of Danzig-Pomerania, together with the territory of Chełmno (Culm) and the bishopric of Warmia (Ermeland) was ceded to Poland by the Order and was then called Royal Prussia, later West Prussia. In the eastern part of the country, later called East Prussia, with Königsberg as its capital, the Order maintained itself, but only by acknowledging their land as a Polish fief for which each succeeding Grand Master had to pay homage to the king. The Prussian state, thereby, lost all its connection, legally somewhat dubious, with the Holy Roman Empire, and the Order had to oblige itself to accept Polish knights within its ranks up to half its total membership. The old and dangerous pressure that the Order had for so long exerted upon Poland as well as upon Lithuania was, it seemed, permanently removed. It was a most gratifying outcome for Poland, in that it freed her for the conduct of a more active policy in relation to Poland's strongly expansionist southern neighbor, Hungary's King Matthias Corvinus.

As long as King George was alive, Casimir had, in the great struggle between George and Matthias, maintained a neutrality friendly to George and had attempted to mediate between the "Hussite king" and the papacy. King George and the Czech Estates had answered Matthias' claim to the Crown of St. Wenceslas by promising the Bohemian succession to Casimir's oldest son, Władysław. But when, at George's death, the young Jagiellon prince was elected and crowned in Bohemia, Matthias, supported by the papacy, decided to contest this decision, and Poland found herself inescapably involved in the bloody struggle over the Czech crown. An attempt by a group of Hungarian barons to overthrow Matthias in favor of one of King Casimir's younger sons, also called Casimir, ended in total failure, but in Bohemia proper young Vladislav II, as he was now called, maintained himself with the help of his father; however, he was unable to regain the dependencies that Matthias held after the conclusion of peace in 1478. Only 12 years later, in 1490, was this abnormal situation removed through Matthias' death and Vladislav's election as his successor. Poland's position now seemed enormously strengthened, as she could expect close cooperation with both of Vladislav's kingdoms. Casimir had also established friendly relations with Emperor Frederick III as well as with his closest neighbor in the West, the Brandenburg Elector Albert Achilles. But in the East, clouds appeared on the horizon.

The danger came from Muscovy. Its Grand Prince, Ivan III, had begun with the systematic process of the "gathering of the Russian lands." In 1471, in a swift war, he had defeated and disarmed, and in 1478 fully annexed, the old city-republic of Novgorod "the Great," and with her huge northern colonial empire more than doubled the extent of his realm. He then turned his attention to Lithuania, whose help had been hoped for in vain by the anti-Muscovite party in Novgorod.

Yet at Casimir's death, in 1492, the Polish-Lithuanian federation had reached the greatest extent it was ever to gain. It was now the largest of all European states. In addition the fact that one of Casimir's sons was now the ruler of another vast area formed by the two kingdoms of Bohemia and Hungary seemed to make the Jagiellon lands an area of invincible strength if they kept together and made the best use of their huge economic resources. In terms of precious metals alone, with Hungary's gold and Bohemia's silver mines, the countries of the "Jagiellon system" should have been able to resist the considerable pressure to which, in the sixteenth century, they were to be exposed. But the Jagiellon lands were too different and their ruling classes too little conscious of their common interests to make for true cooperation, although there was frequent but not always close contact between the brothers.

In the lands of King Vladislav II—Bohemia and Hungary—the advent of the Jagiellon ruler meant an end to the period of vigorous national kingship that had characterized both George of Poděbrady and Matthias Corvinus. In Bohemia it was especially harmful that Vladislav II was after 1490 mostly an absentee ruler. The cities, above all, without whose health and whose active representation in the national diets there could be no internal balance of social relationships and no strength of the crown, were systematically weakened in a long drawn-out struggle in which the gentry, unwisely, sided with the barons. In a series of restrictive laws the peasants were tied to the soil, and again made into serfs—a development paralleled in Poland. In general the Jagiellon period of their history does not present itself as a time of greatness for the Czechs as it does for the Poles. Yet at least one remarkable occurrence has to be mentioned, the roots of which go back to the reign of George but which did not develop fully until the last quarter of the century: the rise of the great reform movement known as the Unity of Czech Brethren.

This second Hussite church (beside the still strongly surviving Utraquists) owed much of its religious ideology to traditions of the earlier, revolutionary Taborite movement but had, under the influence of the great religious thinker Peter Chelčický (ca. 1390-1460), completely abandoned all the violent militancy of the Taborites. Like them, however, the Brethren had cut their ties with the Church of Rome. They tried to establish their own communities in which they would not be forced to take part in the activities of the corrupt world. Especially they refused to take oaths and to participate in war or even in any form of police action. Their combination of pacifism and anarchism had led to their persecution under George of Poděbrady, but under his successor they found protectors among some of the dominant Utraquist barons and, slowly abandoning their radical ban on any participation in political, administrative, and judicial work, they managed to widen enormously the circle of their adherents and to become one of the leading religious communities of the nation. By the time Luther appeared on the scene, Bohemia (and Moravia) had, in the reactivated Utraquist church (later called Neo-Utraquism) and the Church of the Brethren, two reformed churches that represented a great majority of the people. The Lutheran reform work gave the adherents of the two churches whose background was Hussite the strong feeling that finally the religious truths—which had been revealed to themselves a hundred years earlier—were now being accepted also by their neighbors, especially in Germany. And the early success of the Lutheran reform in the two northern dependencies, Lusatia and Silesia, seemed finally to eliminate one of the barriers between them and the ethnically Czech regions in Bohemia and Moravia.

The Reformation seemed to hit fertile ground in Poland also. It was especially in "Royal Prussia," in such cities as Danzig and Toruń, that the movement first struck root, and from here it soon crossed the border into the autonomous state of the Prussian Order, whose Grand Master, the Hohenzollern prince Albert, used this opportunity to secularize the state and to transform it into a duchy with himself as the hereditary duke. King Sigismund I of Poland, the third and youngest of the sons of Casimir IV to wear the Polish crown, agreed to this transformation under the condition that Albert did homage to him and that the duchy was not to come under the rule of the older Brandenburg branch of the house of Hohenzollern.

From Prussia, especially from Königsberg and its newly established university, the Lutheran reformation quickly penetrated into the south and could not be stopped by a long series of royal and ecclesiastical decrees against the German heresy. Nearly two decades after the Lutherans came the first waves of conversion to the reformed (Calvinist) faith. This movement was strengthened by the fact that the greatest of the Protestant reformers of Poland, Jan Łaski (Johannes a Lasco), was a Calvinist. A brilliant man of great religious intensity and a comprehensive Humanist erudition, he abandoned his prebend as a canon of Gniezno cathedral and did much for the reformation movement in Northwest Germany (Friesland) and in England, where Cranmer was one of his friends and, in a way, of his disciples. His later years, after 1556, were devoted to the strengthening of Polish Protestantism and to an attempt, only partly successful, at unifying its various branches.

Besides Lutherans and Calvinists, the Czech Brethren also began to play an increasingly large role when several hundred of them who had been driven out of Bohemia by Ferdinand I in 1548 settled partly in Prussia and to a larger extent in Poland. Teachings of the Czech Brethren as well as of the Anabaptists, who had fled to Poland from the German countries and Moravia, had some influence on one of the most interesting flowerings of the reform spirit in Poland. This was anti-Trinitarianism, at the time also called Arianism by its enemies, and eventually most widely known as Socinianism. During the last four decades of the sixteenth century this movement, with ideas largely stemming from such men as Servetus and Jacob Palaeologus, but further developed by a brilliant Polish thinker, Peter Giezek (Peter Gonesius) challenged the readiness of Polish religious minds to go new ways by giving up the dogma of the Trinity. Everywhere else Unitarian thoughts met with that extreme hostility among Lutherans and Calvinists as well as Catholics that was about to destroy Anabaptism and had martyred Servetus and Palaeologus in Geneva and Rome. In Poland alone, under Sigismund Augustus, a truly tolerant king, it was possible for this new teaching to spread and, at least for a while, to acquire strength and respect. Its center became the town of Raków, already a center of Anabaptism in the 1560s, and there, in the early years of the seventeenth century, largely under the guidance of Faustus Socinus (Sozzini), who had taken over the leadership of the anti-Trinitarian movement during the last two decades of the century, the movement formulated its evangelical rationalism in the Racovian Catechism. From Poland the movement spread to other countries, such as Transylvania, Holland, and Britain, and eventually, though in indirect ways, planted the seeds of the modern Unitarianism that was to attain full growth in nineteenth-century America.

Polish Protestantism reached its greatest strength during the reign of King Sigismund II Augustus (1548-72), the last of the Jagiellons. He was the one Polish king who had genuine sympathy for the reform movement, though he never abandoned the Catholic church, and tried to gain Rome's agreement to many of the reforms demanded by the Estates. In the main, the reform would stand and fall with the nobility. The cities were weak—far weaker than in Bohemia—and the peasantry was much less influenced by the Protestants than the nobility. But throughout the second half of the sixteenth century the dominant spirit in Poland was one of religious tolerance, which made the country appear to be a paradise compared with other parts of Europe where the religious split had resulted in fierce governmental persecution or bloody civil wars.

Even the Counter Reformation, when it came, took rather gentle forms. This was perhaps partly due to the personality of its leader, the great Cardinal Stanisław Hosius, who tried to convince rather than to force, and whose main weapons were, beside the writing of his famous *Confessio fidei catholicae*, the development of a great system of institutes of higher learning, beginning with the establishment of the Jesuit College of Braunsberg. It was partly the surprising success of this educational offensive of the Catholics that gave the Protestants, in the seventh decade of the sixteenth century, the impulse to gain additional strength by unity in the form of two great acts, the "Consensus Sandomiriensis" of 1570 and the "Confederation of Warsaw" of 1573. The "Consensus" was meant to eliminate all friction or struggle between the three Protestant groups, while the "Confederation" bound the Estates and the king to religious toleration and equal status and protection for all the main religious bodies. Yet the last quarter of the century, after the death of Sigismund Augustus, saw a steady weakening of Polish Protestantism. By the turn of the century it seemed doubtful whether Protestantism could even retain a strong foothold in Poland, let alone prevail over Catholicism. In a sense, then, the Polish Reformation was a great episode, admirable above all for the civilized character in which the Polish upper classes—magnates, gentry, and townspeople—managed to resolve their differences without resorting to the bloodshed and harsh inquisitory methods used by the allied state and church powers in almost all other lands, a civilized procedure which by no means indicated a lack of religious fervor.

But if the Reformation remained in the end an episode, the same can certainly not be said of the other great movement with which it was largely contemporary and not unconnected—though it preceded and survived the Reformation and left, as a contribution to national traditions, a more lasting heritage—the Polish Renaissance.

Its beginnings go back to the times of Casimir IV, who had his sons educated by two remarkable men—one a Pole, the brilliant canon (later archbishop) Jan Długosz, who was the one great historian of the late Polish Middle Ages and incidentally an important source for Bohemian and Hungarian as well as Polish history; and the other, from 1470 on, an Italian, the humanist Filippo Buonacorsi who, after Casimir's death, became for some time one of the chief advisers of his successor, King John Albert. It was he who established a regular and lively contact between the Polish court and the great Renaissance centers of Italy. And this process was continued when the youngest of Casimir's sons, Sigismund I, married the highly gifted and ambitious princess Bona Sforza of the ducal house of Milan. With her arrival (she was queen from 1518 to 1548), Italian Renaissance influence multiplied and left deep traces not only in the cultural but even, thanks to her enormous energy, also in the political and economic life of Poland, where she hoped to strengthen the nation as a whole by strengthening the central power of the crown.

The Italian Renaissance influence of Queen Bona's court fell on a highly fertile soil, and the sixteenth century consequently brought forth some of the greatest minds of Polish history. No other light shines as brightly as that of Nicholas Copernicus, an alumnus of Cracow, Bologna, and Padua, a mind of true Renaissance universalism but most influential as a revolutionary astronomer who overthrew the limiting prejudices of the Ptolemaic system. If Copernicus was the greatest scientist, Andrew Frycz Modrzewski was Poland's leading political and legal thinker of the time, a bold reforming spirit in his plans both for the constitution of the Polish state and for some beginning of international order.

But there were also a number of men who, as poets and writers, began to lift the Polish language to the level of a fine and versatile instrument of literary expression. The greatest among them were Nicholas Rey and Jan Kochanowski. Rey (1505-69), a Calvinist, was, in his popular satirical work, sometimes compared with Chaucer. Kochanowski, a generation younger and a member of the Catholic gentry, developed truly great lyrical poetry in Polish, most moving in the "Laments" over the death of a young daughter. Through him and some of his gifted younger successors, Polish literature during the reign of King Sigismund Augustus (whose secretary Kochanowski was) reached a zenith and justified the characterization of this period as a Golden Age.

The reign of Sigismund Augustus was notable for one other reason: it gave the Polish-Lithuanian symbiosis a firm constitutional foundation in the Union of Lublin of 1569. The king had much influence upon the development, yet he would hardly have been able to overcome the resistance in both realms to such a close union if the eastern danger had not become truly threatening. It was personified in the dark figure of Tsar Ivan the Terrible.

The tsar's expansionist experiments in the west had, at an early stage, actually resulted in a gain to the Jagiellon realm—the Baltic region belonging to the now secularized Livonian Order. Its possession, giving Poland a long Baltic coastline, was contested by Brandenburg but her agreement was bought by the dangerous concession that the older, electoral line of the Hohenzollerns could succeed their Prussian cousins if that line became extinct. Another concession—the agreement to Swedish occupation of Estonia—led to a Polish-Swedish alliance against Ivan. Yet the tsar succeeded in further nibbling away ethnically Russian territory that had belonged to the Grand Duchy of Lithuania, especially the region of Polotsk. The Lithuanian gentry, which had long borne the brunt of the border struggle with Muscovy, now insisted on making more sure of Polish support, and strengthened its position vis-à-vis the great magnates by establishing in Lithuania, as had before been established in Poland, the institution of regional parliaments called dietines (*sejmiki*). This institution created the broad basis for the common parliament, henceforth to be elected for the whole realm and thus to be shared by both nations. The chief executive of this great region—until now the king of Poland who had, legally, been considered the suzerain of the grand duke of Lithuania, though in fact both had for a long time been the same person and had thus established a true personal union—was now to be elected by this common parliament as king and grand duke, thus making it impossible for the two constituent parts to dissolve the union. Nevertheless the Grand Duchy retained administrative autonomy, even to the extent of having its own army.

As the Jagiellon dynasty, since the times of its founder Władysław Jagiello, had been in form elective but in fact hereditary in Lithuania, the Union of Lublin with its institution of one common ruler might well have strengthened not only the cohesion of the federation of the two nations but also the position of the dynasty—if only the dynasty had lasted. But Sigismund Augustus had no offspring, and none of his successors was able to establish a firm enough position to free future elections from the unpleasant and destructive implications of competitive offers presented to the nation's nobility by potential candidates.

It was, however, not only the dynastic development that gave the gentry a position of overwhelming strength in the social and political structure of Poland. As in Bohemia so in Poland, too, the noble landowners were able to strengthen their position in relation to the peasantry, whom they thoroughly subjected to their will, depriving them of all rights of changing masters if they wished or of appealing from the jurisdiction of their lord to a higher court, the only exceptions being the peasants on crown and church lands. One of the main impulses for the legislation, enacted by 1532, that destroyed what freedom the peasants had possessed was the great demand in parts of Western Europe for Polish grain, which was shipped down the Vistula from many regions and sent, via Danzig, to its markets. Thus a strong common interest was created among most groups of the Polish nobility for the expansion of arable land and its use for grain growing—a process that made it necessary in the eyes of the gentry to establish as large a pool of dependent labor as possible. In Bohemia, comparable processes had found resistance, for a time, among the strong urban elements, which had their own representation in the diet, but no such resistance existed in Poland and the gentry had its way with little difficulty. Thus it might be said that in terms of the balance of social forces the "Royal Republic," born with the death of the last Jagiellon ruler, Sigismund Augustus, in 1572, already contained the seeds of decay in its very structure.

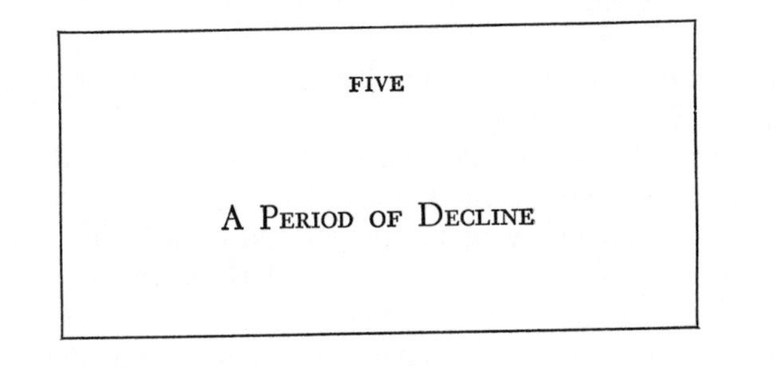

FIVE

A Period of Decline

THE CZECH "STÄNDESTAAT" TO THE TIME OF ECLIPSE

The Jagiellon kings had not done great things for their Kingdom of Bohemia. Yet Louis, for all the weakness of his reign, arising from his personal immaturity and the demanding problems of Hungary, might at least have prevented a further reduction of the royal power, and indeed he made one attempt to do so by supporting the cities against the high nobility. But this, like his whole reign, was no more than an episode. In August 1526, trying to oppose a huge Turkish army with grossly inadequate forces containing neither the approaching Croat nor the promised Bohemian contingents, he and his army succumbed and Hungary lay prostrate before Suleiman the Magnificent. The choice of a new king was much influenced by the Treaty of Vienna, concluded in 1515 between Vladislav II and Maximilian I of Hapsburg and assuring each of the two royal houses the succession in the realm of the other in case of its extinction. This treaty, while not confirmed by the Czech Estates, had been reinforced by the double marriage of Louis with Mary of Hapsburg and of Ferdinand with Anne Jagiello. Louis' death without offspring made Anne and Ferdinand the nearest claimants, and in view of the undiminished Turkish danger Ferdinand, already since 1522 the ruler of the hereditary Hapsburg possessions in Austria, had little difficulty in obtaining the election by the Czech Estates after he had accepted the majority of the conditions presented by the Estates. As Ferdinand I was at the same time elected king of Hungary (though a large part of the country came under Turkish rule and Transylvania under that of a rival Magyar prince, John Zápolya), the year 1526 formed the beginning of the great Hapsburg Empire dominating the Danubian regions of Central and East Central Europe. Therewith also died the idea of a great and united Jagiellon system embracing all of East Central Europe.

For the early Hapsburg rulers up to 1618—as for the later ones—possession of the lands of the Crown of St. Wenceslas was of vital importance. These lands were the richest and most highly developed parts of their heritage, and with so much of Hungary gone—and the Spanish relatives wielding much influence but having their own difficult problems with the Netherlands and France—they could hardly have retained, even less have consolidated, their heritage without this basis, and they certainly could not have financed the almost constant defensive, and eventually offensive, war against the dangerous power of the Crescent. The crucial problem of the Hapsburg kings—all of whom, after the abdication of Charles V, were also Roman Emperors—was, in relation to their Bohemian realm, to strengthen their hold upon this valuable basis without, by this very process, alienating the high nobility, on whom their election had depended and without or against whom it was difficult to maintain their dominion.

On the whole the Hapsburgs, and especially Ferdinand I, did this with skill and fair success. The first difficulties arose in connection with the Schmalkaldic War as the Czech Estates, and especially the city of Prague, rejected Ferdinand's demand that they help the Emperor Charles V in his struggle against Germany's Protestant princes. In his punitive action in 1548 Ferdinand occupied the castle of Prague and had the supposed ringleaders, two knights and two Prague city councillors, but none of the barons, executed. He also seriously restricted the old rights of the capital, a step that found no resistance from, but was rather welcome to, the still powerful magnates. He put much of the blame on the Church of the Czech Brethren, several hundreds of whom were banished and found refuge and a new region for expansion in Ducal Prussia and, above all, in Poland. On the other hand, Ferdinand favored the "Old-Utraquists," the conservative wing of the Hussite church, and even induced Pope Pius IV, in 1564, almost exactly a century after Pius II had outlawed the Compacts and the chalice, to give to all bishops of the Empire the right to grant the chalice to all laymen who asked for it. If this, and his efforts to secure permission for priests to marry, expressed a measure of religious toleration on the part of the first Ferdinand, his son Maximilian II (1564-76) went considerably further. Indeed, he might have gone all the way of accepting some form of Protestantism for himself and his countries—a step that might have changed the course of history—if it had not been for the severe pressure put on him by his Spanish relatives whom, in view of the Turkish dangers, he could not easily neglect. Nonetheless, Maximilian's liberalism toward the Protestant denominations, with the partial exception of the Brethren, worked at times as a brake on the Counter Reformation in the countries of the Bohemian crown as well as in Austria. For the Counter Reformation, led in the Hapsburg countries most vigorously by the brilliant Jesuit Peter Canisius, one of the greatest achievements was the founding in 1555 of a Catholic University in Prague, the Clementinum, which soon proved a successful competitor to the older, Utraquist-dominated Charles University. Only a hundred years later the two institutions were merged into one common, strictly Catholic school, the "Carolo-Ferdinandea." Protestantism, on the other hand, gained some unity and strength when in 1575 the Czech Estates presented to their king, as an expression of the common creed of all Protestant groups in the country, the *Confessio Bohemica*, essentially a combination of the teachings of the Augsburg Confession with those of the Hussite churches, including some of the increasingly Calvinist ideas of the Brethren. Though Maximilian never underwrote the *Confessio Bohemica*, he promised freedom of worship to the Protestants, exempting only later, in a largely ineffectual edict, the Czech Brethren.

The religious as well as the political conflicts of the time came to a head during the long reign (1576-1612) of his eldest son, Rudolf II. A gifted but capricious man, he combined a strong humanistic education and a fervent interest in and understanding for the fine arts and some fields of science with a psychotic distrust of people that eventually developed into a sort of persecution mania. Taking his residence at the great castle of Prague, he soon got into conflict with the predominantly Protestant Estates of Bohemia. But he utterly lacked any competence as a ruler, and this was felt even more distinctly in the dependencies of the Bohemian realm, in Austria, and especially in Hapsburg Hungary, which, in the last decade of the century, suffered from a new outbreak of the border wars with Turkey.

This led to increasing dissatisfaction with the Emperor on the part of the Hapsburg princes—Rudolf's brothers, especially Archduke Matthias, and his cousins—until there was open rebellion and actual warfare. It was this desperate situation that eventually, in 1609, forced Rudolf, though he had all along favored a far more stringent counter reformation, to make decisive concessions to the Protestant Estates of Bohemia. The "Letter of Majesty" signed by Rudolf on July 9, 1609, guaranteed complete freedom of worship to all adherents of the *Confessio Bohemica*, without any regard to their superiors. It returned to the Estates the full control of the Utraquist Consistory and of the Caroline University of Prague, as well as the right to build churches and schools anywhere, whether on lay or on ecclesiastical lands. This last arrangement was also confirmed by an agreement between Catholic and Protestant members of the Estates. Finally the letter confirmed the institution of "defensores," of defenders of the faith, to be appointed by the Estates.

The Letter of Majesty seemed, at the time, to be a great success for Bohemian Protestantism. But in fact it was mostly a defensive measure, much needed in view of the steadily growing strength and aggressiveness of the counterreform movement that enjoyed the full support of all the Hapsburg princes, and quite especially of Archduke Ferdinand, who had managed, in the years around the turn of the century, to purge by the most violent means the Duchy of Styria of all Protestants. When, in 1612, Rudolf's enforced abdication called his childless brother Matthias to the throne, Ferdinand became the heir presumptive and did not scruple to promise that he would respect the Letter of Majesty while fully determined to destroy the Czech heretics as he had destroyed those in Styria. The Bohemian Estates should have been well aware of this yet they accepted him in 1617 as their future king. He was even crowned.

The great collision occurred in May 1618. After several other breaches of the Letter of Majesty, the Protestant Estates remonstrated vigorously when two churches built in the small towns of Broumov (Braunau) and Hrob (Klostergrab) were closed and one of them torn down, by order of the Broumov abbot and the Archbishop of Prague. The Emperor tried to forbid further protest demonstrations by the Estates, or by the "defensores." Bohemia's Protestant leaders, aware that both Matthias and his crowned successor

Ferdinand intended to go to extremes in crushing all opposition, began to plan a rebellion, directed against the Emperor's lieutenants in Prague. On May 23, 1618, a group of more than 100 members of the Estates, led by Count Thurn, attacked two of Matthias' leading Czech councillors, William Slavata and Jaroslav Martinic and, declaring them traitors, threw them out of a window of the Prague castle into the moat. (They survived the fall.) The "defenestration" was the signal for a more general movement. The Estates elected a provisional government of 30 "directors," 10 from each of the Estates. Hopes for any peaceful solution dwindled fast, especially when the Emperor's compromise-minded chief minister, Cardinal Khlesl, was removed by Ferdinand, who followed Matthias on the throne in March 1619.

The Estates were now determined to find another king. Of three potential candidates, the Duke of Savoy, the Lutheran Elector of Saxony, and the Calvinist Elector of the Palatinate, they decided, in August 1619, on the last named. As head of the Protestant Union of German princes and a son-in-law of King James I of England he was expected to be able to muster strong support. Elector Frederick accepted. But he was neither a strong personality in his own right, nor did he receive the expected support, as King James hoped and worked for a closer relationship with the Spanish Hapsburgs. There were only some subsidies from the Netherlands and some quite effective military help from Gábor Bethlen, Prince of Transylvania. Unfortunately his activities were severely hampered by King Sigismund III Vasa of Poland, who felt obliged, by an invasion of Transylvania, to help the Catholic Hapsburgs against the Protestant Czechs.

In the war which meantime had begun, the Czech army, under Thurn's command, had first taken the offensive, had invaded Austria, where the revolt had strong sympathy among the Protestant members of the Estates, and had even hoped to conquer Vienna, which was only saved for Ferdinand by the last minute arrival of new troops under Spanish command. But from then on the military initiative fell into the hands of the imperialist side, with Duke Maximilian of Bavaria, the head of the Catholic League of German princes and a far abler man than his cousin Frederick, playing a leading role. His chief general, the Belgian Count Tilly, led the combined Catholic forces into Bohemia and achieved, on November 8, a quick and decisive victory over the Bohemian army at the so-called White Mountain, a hill just to the west of Prague. The principal reason for the defeat was the fact that the Bohemian troops, mainly mercenaries, had long been left unpaid and were in a mood of mutiny, while the imperialist troops were well paid and well fed. This, however, does not explain the subsequent surrender, without any fight, of the city of Prague and the utter collapse of resistance throughout the lands of the Bohemian crown. The headlong flight of King Frederick and his whole court had something to do with it, but more important was the fact that here was no longer a nation consciously and courageously defending its liberty as the Czechs had done, against far greater odds, 200 years earlier. Instead the fight was mainly directed by a poorly organized nobility trying to defend, along with its religious liberty, its privileges and its paramount position, while the masses of the people in town and country, but especially the oppressed peasantry, had little to gain in risking their lives for the maintenance of a largely unjust and unhealthy social structure. These people could hardly grasp the terrible consequences that the defeat of 1620 was to inflict upon the whole Czech nation.

The victor's vengeance was grim. It began with the arrest, in February 1621, of all leaders of the revolution who had not fled in time. Twenty-seven of them, the majority Czechs, but also a considerable number of Protestant Germans, were executed on June 21 in front of the city hall on the Old Town Square, and their heads were exhibited for years on one of the bridge towers. Among them was the Rector of the Charles University, Johannes Jessenius, a famous physician and brilliant scientist, whose tongue was cut out before he was decapitated.

More important was the confiscation of all possessions of nobles and townsmen held to have been involved in the revolt or unwilling to be converted to Catholicism. A mass emigration followed which has few parallels in European history prior to the twentieth century. It appears that by 1628 some 36,000 families, representing somewhere between 150,000 and 200,000 individuals, had left Bohemia, and that the value of the confiscated land represented the astronomic figure of at least 100 million gulden, or nearly three-quarters of all the land. The emigrants included the very cream of the Czech nation. Some of them went only as far as neighboring Saxony and later took part in those phases of the Thirty Years' War in which, under Swedish leadership, the attempt was made to liberate the country. Many, however, went farther away. Few ever returned. The rich flowering of Czech culture, especially nurtured through much of the sixteenth century by the humanistic developments within the Church of the Brethren, was effectively destroyed, and with it much of the wealth and sophistication of the Czech language and literature. All printed works now came under the strict censorship of the Jesuits, who allowed little to be published that was not meant to support directly their work of mass conversion. One of them later boasted to have burned no less than 60,000 Czech books. This fanatical destruction of Czech publications did not only deal a well-nigh fatal blow to all literature and higher education in Czech in Bohemia and Moravia but had also its effects in the Slovak regions of Hungary, where the Hapsburgs continued to rule and where Czech books, among them the beautiful Czech translation of the Scripture, the so-called Kralice Bible, had been fully accepted by the Slovak middle class and had contributed a good deal to the strengthening of Slovak literary activity.

Among the many fine minds—religious and political leaders, authors, scholars, and artists—that were lost to the Bohemian lands, though by no means to the Czech cultural tradition, the greatest was John Amos Komenský or Comenius, a Moravian of universal knowledge and erudition, encyclopedist, philosopher, poet, theologian, a fervent advocate of ecumenical cooperation, and also the last Bishop of the Old Church of the Brethren. His highest merit was his fundamental reform of the main principles and ideas of education, which made him the first great philosopher of education and which has retained its significance to our days. His fate drove him through many countries—Poland, Germany, eastern Hungary, England, Sweden, and the Netherlands. At one time the young Harvard College tried to lure him to New England, but he refused. His influence reaches from Leibniz to Goethe, Herder, Masaryk, and John Dewey.

This fierce destruction of a high and noble civilization is surely one of the darkest aspects in the political history of the Counter Reformation. And the heirs of all this enormous robbery—some Catholic Czechs, but mostly foreigners, Germans, Spaniards, Italians, and Walloons who had served the Emperor and were now amply rewarded—contributed their part to the denationalization of the ruling elements of Bohemia and in particular of Prague. Perhaps the one redeeming feature of this process was that the new owners, amply enriched, proceeded, some of them long before the end of the Thirty Years' War, to establish their new magnificence by the erection of gorgeous palaces, especially in Prague. They did their share, thus, in adding to the architectural greatness of Bohemian Gothic the splendor of the Baroque Age. In time some of those great lords did acquire, in addition to their status as members of the Hapsburg court nobility, some Bohemian qualities. But essentially they contributed to an atmosphere that, while not lacking a good deal of sophistication, had little to do with the great traditions of the country. Those had to be regained, after a long period of hibernation, from newly awakening forces outside or below the aristocracy.

Meantime the great war went on, no longer just a struggle for or against Bohemia's religious and political freedom. One of the most important figures of this confused and seemingly endless struggle was a gifted and ambitious Czech nobleman who had early been converted from the Church of the Brethren to Roman Catholicism—Albert of Waldstein, usually called Wallenstein. As creator and commander in chief of the Emperor's own army he contributed to the sequence of Catholic victories, but the very degree to which he thereby strengthened Ferdinand's position led to strong resistance against him among the German princes, Catholic as well as Protestant, and to his dismissal in 1630. Meantime he had established a large part of northern Bohemia as his personal domain—the Duchy of Friedland—whose economic potential he developed, in the short time left to him, to an astonishing degree. When Gustavus Adolphus of Sweden rallied Protestant Germany and turned the tide, Ferdinand had to recall Wallenstein, giving him extraordinary military and political powers. Late in 1631, the Saxons had, with strong strategic support from the Swedes, liberated Prague, where they were greeted with enthusiasm by the Protestants. This happiness did not last long; in May 1632 Wallenstein reconquered the city, and Bohemia was again at his disposal. But from now on he seemed to procrastinate and indeed began to negotiate with the Swedes, both before and after Gustavus' death at Lützen. For a time he hoped, so it seems, to gain the crown of Bohemia for himself, but in the end he began to lose control over his army and, by a vacillating policy, played into the hands of his enemies, who had him murdered at Cheb (Eger) in February 1634.

Bohemia was once more invaded by the Swedes, and once more Prague was besieged and attacked by a Swedish—Protestant—army. But this was in July 1648, at the very end of the war, 30 years after the outbreak of the rebellion of the Bohemian Estates, at a time when the Peace of Westphalia had almost been concluded. This time there were hardly any Protestants left in Prague to greet the would-be liberators, and the great majority of the people showed more readiness to defend the city against the Swedes than the Praguers had done 28 years earlier against the imperial army.

The dreadfully devastated and depopulated Kingdom of Bohemia, indeed, was securely in the possession of the Hapsburgs again, as were Moravia and Silesia, whereas Lusatia, by the peace terms, was ceded to the Elector of Saxony. The kingdom, from then on, was governed entirely from Vienna, where, on the basis of a new constitution, the "Vernewerte Landesordnung," a Bohemian chancery, was established. The influence of the Estates was much reduced. The office of Lord High-Burgrave who, in the king's absence, had been the kingdom's governor, was abolished. These were effective steps in the process of centralizing the administration and of turning the Kingdom of Bohemia into a mere province of the Hapsburg lands.

THE ROYAL REPUBLIC

It was in the main a decision of the Czech high nobility, the great magnates, that in 1526 had called a Hapsburg upon the throne of Bohemia. In 1572, after the death of Sigismund Augustus of Poland, the Polish magnates would also have liked to elect a Hapsburg, but the great masses of the *szlachta*, the gentry, led by the gifted young lawyer Jan Zamoyski, outvoted the magnates—insisting on equal votes for all members of the nobility—and elected Henry of Valois, the third son of Catherine de Medici, dowager queen of France. Henry had to pay for this with far-reaching concessions that enormously strengthened the influence of Polish parliamentarism. The king had to oblige himself to call the *Sejm* at least every second year and not to try to name his successor or to marry without the consent of Parliament. He had regularly to consult with the four-man committee of a privy council appointed not by him but by Parliament. Henry, as henceforth all his successors, accepted the articles, arrived in Poland and was crowned, but within half a year, upon the news of the death of his brother, King Charles IX, he escaped from Poland to mount the French throne. His successor became, against strong Hapsburg bids, the vigorous young prince of Transylvania, Stephen Báthory, who was married to Anne, one of the sisters of the last Jagiellon king.

In his short reign (1576-86) Stephen proved to be a superb statesman, military organizer, and general. He rebuilt Poland's armed forces, suppressed a rebellion of Danzig, and answered Ivan's IV invasion of Livonia with an offensive war against Muscovy (1579-81), which forced the "terrible" tsar to give up all his western conquests. Under his brilliant leadership Poland-Lithuania was still the foremost power of Central and Eastern Europe. There also were some badly needed financial, judicial, and administrative reforms, but the young king had no time to regain permanently that necessary strength for the royal office which, as long as he lived, emerged from his powerful personality.

The general trend throughout the decades following the disappearance of the Jagiellons went in favor of an ever-growing influence of the Parliament (*Sejm*), and within Parliament of the great masses of the lower nobility, the gentry, which in the course of the sixteenth century succeeded in gaining the upper hand in relation to the magnates on one side, the towns (which had never achieved a paramount role) on the other side. Already in 1505, still at the height of Jagiellon rule, had the Statute *Nihil novi* established the principle that no constitutional changes should ever occur without permission of the councillors (senators) and the deputies from the various districts. As these, however, were bound to present the decisions which, after discussing the king's suggestions, the gentry had made in their district assemblies, the dietines, or *sejmiki*, the members of the lower nobility could generally determine the course of events, at least as far as legislation was concerned. Even in the sixteenth century the principle had been established that decisions by the national Parliament had to be unanimous, at least insofar as the *Sejm*-marshal (speaker) did not find any contradiction in summing up what he considered the sense of the house. Small capricious vetoes hardly occurred at this stage and could normally be overcome by persuasion or, occasionally, threats from powerful majorities. If substantial minorities remained in opposition and no acceptance could be gained within 6 weeks of sessions the *Sejm* was dissolved and all its work became invalid. Even this, however, was a rare enough occurrence during the sixteenth century. This period was thus dominated by a system of legislative (and to some extent even executive) government by consent in which a relatively high proportion of the people—the gentry included probably one tenth of the total population—could participate. While in modern terms this must still be considered as a sort of oligarchy, and while there seems to be little justification for using the word democracy, it is yet remarkable that a nobility that contained thousands of small, often very small, landholders maintained the principles of political equality within their class and could resist so successfully the general trend toward princely absolutism that dominated, with hardly any exceptions, the whole European continent. It is tempting, to some extent, to compare Polish and British parliamentarism, and it is obvious that the survival of the latter into modern times is at least partly due to England's insular position, which made it, even in times of weakness, much less open to invasion than Poland. On the other hand, the vigor of English parliamentarism, based, as in Poland, largely upon the rule of a powerful gentry, was also characterized by the general alliance of this class with the urban middle class, an alliance that made a most successful use of the development of capitalism and an early industrial revolution. In Poland the opposite was true. The gentry—in all its parts, from the well-to-do barons to the small freeholders boasting a coat-of-arms—fought hard against any attempt of the cities to gain influence or even maintain whatever modest influence some of the largest cities such as the capitals Cracow and Warsaw ever had. Furthermore, the position of the peasantry deteriorated in the sixteenth century much as it did in Bohemia; a new era of serfdom followed.

While there were not in Poland, as in seventeenth-century England, open rebellions of the politically organized gentry against the king, the Polish gentry did not have to take such steps in order to limit and reduce royal power. This could be done so much more easily as a result of the elective character of the Polish crown.

In 1587, as some time before or later, the question arose how to avoid the election of one of the Hapsburgs, who always had a clique of magnates and much money working for them. Owing to vigorous interference of Chancellor Zamoyski—still, as during the last two elections, the most powerful among the country's political figures—Archduke Maximilian, the younger brother of the Emperor, was eliminated and the son of John III, king of Sweden, and of Catherine Jagiello, sister of Sigismund II and of Stephen Báthory's widow Anne, was elected and crowned. Apart from his Jagiellon blood the expectation of a personal union and therefore also of close cooperation with Sweden, already the strongest power of the Baltic, had seemed to make the choice a wise one. In fact, Sigismund's foreign policy was a series of catastrophic mistakes, the worst of them resulting from his claims to be king both of Poland and, from the death of his father in 1592, of Sweden. He was a convert to Catholicism, trying to do to Sweden what Mary Tudor had tried to do to England four decades earlier. But Protestantism had struck much deeper roots in late sixteenth-century Sweden than in mid-sixteenth-century England, and Sigismund's attempted counterreformation merely resulted in his being deposed in Sweden in 1599 in favor of his uncle, Charles IX. Sigismund, however, was unwilling to accept defeat, and the dynastic struggle between the two branches of the house of Vasa was maintained, in a sequence of wars, to the peace of Oliva of 1660. Most of it was fought on Polish soil, and in the outcome Poland lost not only Livonia but was much weakened at a time when she needed her strength to deal with dangers threatening from the east.

During the early years of the seventeenth century it may indeed have looked as if the Muscovite giant, shaken by convulsions largely due to the effects of the reign of Ivan the Terrible, was going to be an easy victim for an aggressive Polish policy. The "False Dimitri," a man claiming to be the long-dead youngest son of Ivan, and married to the daughter of a Polish magnate, was recognized as tsar in Moscow, which he opened to strong Polish influence. The anti-Polish party in Muscovy, led by Vasily Shuisky, thereupon allied itself with Charles of Sweden. Sigismund was lucky enough to have in Hetman Stanisław Żółkiewski one of the best military minds in Polish history at his disposal. Żółkiewski's victory over Shuisky resulted in the acceptance by a strong group of the Moscow boyars of Sigismund's son

THE POLISH-LITHUANIAN
and BOHEMIAN KINGDOMS
at the Beginning of the
SEVENTEENTH CENTURY
0
100
200
MILES
Gulf of Riga
Riga
COURLAND
MUSCOVY
GRAND DUCHY OF LITHUANIA
Baltic Sea
Königsberg
Danzig
ROYAL PRUSSIA
DUCAL PRUSSIA
Vilna
Dvina
Smolensk
Dnepr
Niemen
Desna
GERMANY
GREAT POLAND
Gniezno
Poznań
Vistula
MASOVIA
Warta
Warsaw
Bug
Pripet
VOLHYNIA
KINGDOM OF POLAND
LUSATIA
SILESIA
Breslau
Oder
Prague
BOHEMIA
Kutná Hora
Vltava
LITTLE POLAND
Cracow
Vistula
Kiev
Lwów
MORAVIA
Brno
PODOLIA
Dnepr
Bug
Danube
HUNGARY
Vienna
Bratislava
(Pressburg)
TURKISH HUNGARY
TRANSYLVANIA
AUSTRIA
HABSBURG HUNGARY
Buda
MOLDAVIA
Black Sea
Sea of Azov
M.B.

Władysław as tsar. But Sigismund insisted that he himself be recognized as tsar and, when the Russians declined, occupied large parts of Russia. For a while a Polish garrison maintained itself in the Kremlin, and Smolensk was conquered, but in the outcome, the Polish occupation, and the contemptuous treatment of the Russians by Sigismund and some of his officials, challenged Russian patriotism and led to the convention of the national assembly (*Zemsky Sobor*) of 1613 which put Tsar Michael of the house of Romanov on the Russian throne. Sigismund's irresponsible eastern adventure contributed much to the awakening of Polonophobia as a basis of Russian nationalism.

The next grave mistake made by Sigismund occurred in the beginning of the Thirty Years' War when, for religious reasons, he decided to help the Emperor Ferdinand II against the revolution of the Bohemian Estates and sent an army against the Transylvanian prince Gábor Bethlen, the only European ruler who had brought effective help to Bohemia. This had a strong impact upon the early development, so catastrophic for the Czechs, of the Thirty Years' War. The invasion of territories considered in Constantinople as a Turkish protectorate led to a dangerous war between Turkey and Poland, which added to the burden of Poland's other military commitments, especially those against Sweden. Thus, in order to prevent a close alliance between Brandenburg and Sweden, and to obtain from the Brandenburg elector George William subsidies for the war against Turkey, Sigismund confirmed him in his claim to the ducal throne of Prussia after the extinction in 1618 of the Albertinian line of the Hohenzollerns. Even though Polish suzerainty was formally maintained, the personal union between Brandenburg and Prussia, the decisive step toward the growth of the later Prussian state, was a most dangerous development for Poland. Despite this sacrifice, the war against Sweden took an unfavorable turn for Poland, especially when in 1611 Charles IX was followed by his brilliant son Gustavus II Adolphus, who carried hostilities, after the conquest of Livonia, on to Polish territory. This phase of the extended struggle with Sweden was ended in 1629 with the treaty of Altmark, which left Gustavus Adolphus in possession of all his gains and enabled him to enter, in full force, the Thirty Years' War on the side of the German Protestants. More than anything else, this treaty proved the hopelessness of Sigismund's foreign policy which had squandered Poland's by no means inexhaustible resources in the service of his dynastic pride and of his ambition to be the great sword-bearer of the Counter Reformation.

Sigismund's work to expand the orbit of the Roman church made one gain that had a wider support among the people of Poland and Lithuania than most of his military adventures. This was, referring back to the Council of Florence, the encouragement and final sanction of the reunification of Catholic and Greek Orthodox Christians in the eastern regions of the Royal Republic, especially in the Polish Ukraine. By the Union of Brześć (Brest-Litovsk), established in 1596 through negotiations between the Polish hierarchy and some of the leading churchmen of the Greek Orthodox Church, a considerable part of the Russian and Ukrainian population of those districts joined the Church of Rome under what appeared to be highly liberal terms —there was to be no radical change in the old eastern ritual. Services would be conducted, as before, in Church Slavonic. The marriage of priests was permitted, as was the use of the chalice for laymen. The Uniat clergy was to be equal in every regard to the Catholic, as long as it recognized the position of the Pope. The Union was ratified by the Pope as well as by Sigismund, and though it had the strong support also of the Jesuits, it seems doubtful whether in any Catholic country with a less developed tradition of religious tolerance such an arrangement would have been possible at this time. In the longer run, however, it did not work out as well as had been hoped. The Moscow Patriarchate soon attacked the Uniats as traitors to the Eastern Church, but in Poland, too, they did not always find the recognition they had expected, and the Uniat bishops did not receive the promised seats in the Senate (Upper house) of the *Sejm*. There was, therefore, a not inconsiderable movement of return to the Russian Orthodox Church, though the Uniat church as such has survived in some strength, both inside and outside Poland, to this day.

After Sigismund's death in 1632 his son, Władysław IV, in many ways a better and more popular ruler than his father, followed without struggle. More realistic than Sigismund, he almost immediately dropped all claims to the Russian throne but maintained those to Sweden, which seemed to become more hopeful when Gustavus Adolphus died without a male heir. But his greatest ambition—to organize a huge crusade against the Turks—also led to his greatest defeat. He had hoped to use, for his planned offensive, the host of the

Zaporozhian Cossacks, some of whom Poland had previously—as so-called registered Cossacks—used in fights against the Crimean Tartars. Large numbers, however, were never "registered." Many of them were former serfs on estates of the Polish grandees or of Polonized Ukrainian nobles. In addition most of them resented the attempt to force them to join the Uniat church. Thus the Ukrainian Cossacks became increasingly hostile to the Polish domination. Under the leadership of the energetic and ambitious hetman Bogdan Khmelnitsky they rebelled against the Polish rule in 1648, just before Władysław's death, massacred thousands of Poles and even larger numbers of Jews, and managed to defeat two Polish armies sent against them by Władysław and his brother and successor John Casimir (1648-68). In 1654 Khmelnitsky put the Cossack people, and with them the Ukraine, under the protection of Tsar Alexis. It is true that Moscow never fully kept the promises of a far-reaching autonomy for the Ukrainian people, and that in the following centuries Ukrainian patriotism and nationalism frequently took a strong anti-Russian color. But the chance for a great Slavic state which would include Poles, Lithuanians, and Ukrainians in a freely cooperative federation was lost under the last Vasas, and Poland's position grew progressively worse under the simultaneous pressure exerted by the two great powers of the East. As yet it was by no means sure that Turkey's power was waning, while Russia was clearly gaining strength. It was due only to the last great personality on the Polish throne that Turkey's weakness was openly established and that she was pressed back from her farthest expansion into Central Europe—John Sobieski, who dominated the Polish scene through most of the last quarter of the seventeenth century (1674-96). He was a truly national king who gained his backing in the field, when in 1673, as "crown general," he destroyed a great Ottoman army which, after occupying the whole Ukraine, had entered Podolia. Though generally trying to maintain Poland's strength by cultivating her relationship to France he was forced by continuing Turkish encroachments to conclude an alliance with Vienna, hoping to form a wider "Holy League" against the still menacing Crescent. When, in 1683, a huge Turkish army beleaguered Vienna, the Polish king came to the rescue and, in close cooperation with the imperial commander, Prince Charles of Lorraine, relieved Vienna and helped in driving the Turks out of Central Hungary. He failed, however, in his attempt to regain Polish suzerainty over Moldavia, and, like Stephen Báthory, was unsuccessful in his attempt to strengthen the crown against the *szlachta*. The nobility now began to fight, all too successfully, for a "freedom" most drastically characterized by the growing use of the *liberum veto*, which tended to stifle all constructive political work, especially legislation. As some members of the *Sejm*, factions as well as individuals, were open to bribes, this gave foreign powers an effective means of influencing Polish policy, including the choice of rulers. It is in this way that it was possible to put German princes, the electors of Saxony, on the Polish throne, twice by dethroning a far better Polish king whom the majority of the nation would have preferred. But even this Polish national king, Stanisław I Leszczyński, owed his election only to the energetic backing of the young Swedish conqueror Charles XII, who had retaliated for the participation of the first Polish king of the Saxon line, Augustus II (the Strong), in the Great Northern War by driving this politically incompetent voluptuary out of Poland. Thereby, it seemed, the endless Polish-Swedish struggle had found an end. But Charles's defeat at the hands of Peter I of Russia led to Stanisław's expulsion and Augustus' return, essentially as Peter's viceroy. On Augustus' death Stanisław, now the father-in-law of Louis XV, was reelected, but again Russia, supported by Austria, interfered, and the War of the Polish Succession (1733-35) ended with his second expulsion and the restoration of the Saxon claimant (Augustus III, 1734-63), whose utter weakness was demonstrated by the way in which, during the Seven Years' War, Russian troops marched without either permission or hindrance back and forth through Poland.

The last Polish King, Stanisław II Poniatowski, was, much like the earlier Stanisław, a man of high gifts, of truly humanist interests and of genuine patriotism. His was the tragic fate to rule the country during a phase of splendid renewal and yet to be unable to prevent its destruction.

A TALE OF FOUR PARTITIONS

The famous Pragmatic Sanction—which gave Emperor Charles VI the right to pass on his dynastic heritage to his daughter—was dutifully accepted by the Bohemian Estates in 1720, yet when, twenty years later, the young Maria Theresa mounted the throne of Bohemia and Hungary, Europe exploded in the Wars of the Austrian Succession, and the feelings of the Bohemian people were shown to be by no means as devoutly loyal to the dynasty as the Estates had claimed. In November 1741, when Elector Charles Albert of Bavaria succeeded, with his own and French troops, in conquering Prague, he was acknowledged as king of Bohemia by a considerable sector of the Estates and the nobility, even before his election as Emperor in January. This, however, remained an episode. Already in 1742 his ally, Frederick II of Prussia, having conquered Bohemia's great northern dependency of Silesia, concluded with Maria Theresa the Peace of Breslau and Berlin by which, as queen of Bohemia, she ceded most of this important country to Prussia. This decision, maintained in the Second Silesian War, and above all in the Seven Years' War, deprived the Bohemian crown of one of its richest provinces. The kingdom itself, however, remained firmly in Hapsburg hands. The Bohemian realm had to contribute more to the financing of the great war than any other part of the monarchy, although it had suffered far more destruction than any other Austrian province. When Maria Theresa's son Joseph II acquired influence, first as his mother's co-ruler, and as absolute ruler after her death in 1780, conditions in the country made it possible for the Czech nation to start on her long, difficult renaissance. As so often in the past, the issue of religious freedom played a role of importance.

When Joseph II, in 1781, issued his famous edict of toleration, he did not act out of special sympathy for the Czechs. Yet among them, more than elsewhere, Protestantism, despite all efforts of the Counter Reformation, had subterraneously survived as a vigorous minority that was to play a leading role in the Czech national renaissance. To a considerable extent this was also true of the Slovaks in Hungary. The fact that Joseph, the very personification of enlightened despotism, tried to force, in the service of administrative centralization, the German language on all nationalities of the Hapsburg Empire in the end only strengthened the response of a reawakening Czech national consciousness. The beginnings of the growth of a new middle class began to contribute to this process, as did, in other ways, the partial abolition of serfdom which made the peasant population more movable and created improved preconditions for the rise of industrial capitalism. Joseph, though at an early time harboring agrarian reform plans, might not have gone as far in trying to liberate the peasants if he had not been shaken up by a great peasant rebellion that erupted in many parts of Bohemia in March 1775 and could only be suppressed by the employment of strong military forces.

Joseph II was the most progress-minded among contemporary rulers, but in his foreign policy he was as eager for military glory and territorial aggrandizement as his two neighbors, Frederick II of Prussia and Catherine II of Russia. His unwillingness to let Russia make still larger gains in Turkey threatened to lead to a collision between the Hapsburg Empire and Russia, and provided the opportunity for Frederick II to suggest, as a way out of this difficulty, that both countries—and his own—should seek compensation by gaining Polish territory. After negotiations during which Maria Theresa's reluctance was overcome by Joseph's healthy appetite, the first partition was forced upon Poland by her three neighbors in 1772. At this stage, Catherine—who had really hoped to gain the whole of Poland at least as an exclusive Russian sphere of influence—seemed to be satisfied with a seemingly modest gain; she received the long narrow strip of land inhabited mostly by Russians and Byelorussians, east of the Dnieper, the Beresina, and the western Dvina. The Hapsburgs obtained, together with parts of "Red Russia" and Podolia—that is, largely Ukrainian territory—also the entirely Polish western Galicia, much of which had belonged to "Little Poland," with lands in the immediate vicinity of Poland's old capital of Cracow. Relatively most profitable was the gain of Prussia. It was old eastern Pomorze, called "Royal Prussia" after 1466 and for more than three centuries Poland's only safe access to the Baltic, since the coast of the dependent Duchy of Kurland had neither good ports nor good connections with central Poland. True, Poland was to keep Danzig and free navigation on the Vistula, but even so she was weakened by this cession to about the same extent that Prussia was strengthened.

Nevertheless the amputation of the three regions had not injured the nation fatally. It was still a large country with great resources, and the first partition seemed the very thing needed to alert and energize all those elements in Polish society that felt the need to reform the country.

It is perhaps incorrect to date this process of moral, educational, and political reform and rejuvenation only from the time of the First Partition. But this painful event gave additional urgency to the understanding of a need which had been recognized by some sensitive patriotic minds before. Most of them had contact with and received inspiration from the movement of the Enlightenment, especially in its French forms. Some help to this development was given when the former king, Stanisław Leszczyński, who after France's defeat in the War of the Polish Succession had been given the Duchy of Lorraine as a compensation, assembled at his court many young Poles eager to serve the cause of reform and even founded a college for Poles at Lunéville. The need to free Polish education from the strict monopoly that, during the seventeenth century, had been gained by the Jesuits was great. The most active representative of the idea of an enlightened educational reform was Stanisław Konarski, originally a Piarist priest, who in 1740 founded in Warsaw a "Collegium Nobilium," not because of prejudice against other classes but because he felt that the gentry from whom, for better or worse, would have to come the political leadership in these critical times, needed above all a better and especially a more scientific education.

But Konarski did not limit himself to educational problems. He took part in a thorough study of Polish law and the Polish constitution and in 1760 began publishing a work of critical examination of the Polish political system, in which he attacked with deadly sharpness and conviction much of the parliamentary practice, especially the *liberum veto*. The work had strong influence already in the actual development, prior to the First Partition, of parliamentary attitudes.

An even more direct influence in preparing for the great reform work eventually done by the Four Years' Diet was exerted by Stanisław Staszic. In a book on the great sixteenth-century statesman Zamoyski and in some political pamphlets he presented a series of suggestions for the reform of Poland's political and social structure, many of which were accepted by the diet. He was also especially interested in the development of the Polish peasantry whom, by the founding of agricultural cooperatives, he hoped to educate into free farmers.

The most colorful figure among those Polish pioneers of reform was Hugo Kołłątaj. Like Konarski he began by tackling problems of education. He succeeded in many constructive changes in the University of Cracow, and when, in 1773, a Commission of National Education was set up, it largely followed his suggestions in reforming and improving the school system of the country. But, unlike most of the other representatives of what might be called the Polish Enlightenment, Kołłątaj was a political fighter who was ready to expose himself in the struggle for a reformed Poland. Thus his role was not limited to the Four Year Parliament and its preparation but was no less influential when, after the Second Partition, the rising against the occupying powers took the form of a real revolution in which Kołłątaj became the leading figure of Polish Jacobinism, a "sin" for which he had to spend much time in Austrian prisons.

Beside these enlightened leaders, the king must not be forgotten or underrated. He had been ever so careful not to antagonize his great protectress, Catherine II, who had once been his mistress but long continued to be his political master. Together with the strong party of the Czartoryskis he had tried to gain Russian approval for all his patriotic plans, but during the years of the late 1780s he convinced himself that by playing the great neighbors one against another and meantime pushing through a vast reform work Poland could still be saved and would again play an important role in European politics. This seemed all the more possible as by now Poland's most determined enemy, Frederick II of Prussia, had died and his successor, Frederick William II, posed as Poland's friend.

It is in these fateful yet hopeful years that King Stanisław displayed real abilities of leading and organizing, which were not limited to the development of an adequate national system of education. During the years from 1788 to 1792, the so-called Four-Years' Parliament worked out a constitution which, had it but had a chance of prolonged implementation, might have mobilized the nation's inherent strength to make her a less easy and less tempting victim to her rapacious neighbors. This famous constitution, accepted on May 3, 1791, turned the Royal Republic into a hereditary parliamentary monarchy which, much like the French constitution of 1790, followed in many ways the English model. Above all it replaced the *liberum veto* by a system of simple majority decision. Unfortunately, attempts to abolish serfdom had been defeated, a circumstance which reduced the readiness of the Polish peasantry to defend with any vigor the new status. But at least the cities received representation and self-government.

Even so this peaceful revolution seemed an outrage to Catherine II —all the more because the reforming groups in the Sejm, as well as

King Stanisław, had been especially encouraged in their work by the Prussian ambassador. Under the diplomatic leadership of Count Hertzberg, Prussia had, early in 1790, concluded a treaty of alliance with Poland which was clearly directed against Russia—a Russia prevented to act in Poland as she was still embroiled in war against Turkey. But this war came to an end, and meantime Prussia and Austria had become entangled in a conflict with revolutionary France. Thus, by 1792, Catherine regained her freedom of action and, making use of a small camarilla of Polish magnates, organized in the "Confederation of Targowica," invaded the country supposedly to protect old Polish liberties against the tyranny of the Warsaw parliament. Prussia, very far from fulfilling her treaty obliging her to defend Poland against Russia's aggression, shamelessly joined in the slaughter of her neighbor and ally. This time the Russian booty was huge, including much of Lithuania and most of the western Ukraine, as well as regions settled by Poles, notably in western Podolia. Prussia swallowed all of Great Poland with Poznania, but also the long coveted cities of Danzig and Toruń. Prussia, thereby, became a state with a large Polish population of nearly two millions. Austria, this time, abstained.

If the Polish patriots, after the First Partition, had tried, with some success, to make the best of a dangerous situation, and had created a Poland that, if allowed to exist, would have been a viable political unit, this could not be repeated after the rape of 1793. Against the Russian occupation of Poland a widespread rebellion broke out in March 1794, and a largely improvised Polish army, brilliantly led by Tadeusz Kościuszko, gained some remarkable victories, partly due to the final liberation of the peasantry by the leaders of the movement. But in October a vastly superior Russian army under Suvorov defeated Kościuszko and the movement collapsed.

The consequence was that now Poland disappeared altogether from the map of Europe. Again, as in the Second Partition, Russia got the lion's share—all the lands east of the Bug and north of the Niemen, including Kurland. The rest, mostly ethnically Polish territories, was divided between Austria, which received the south with Cracow, and Prussia which gained the north with Warsaw. Never in the history of Europe had a whole, large nation been wiped out in this brutal and callous manner.

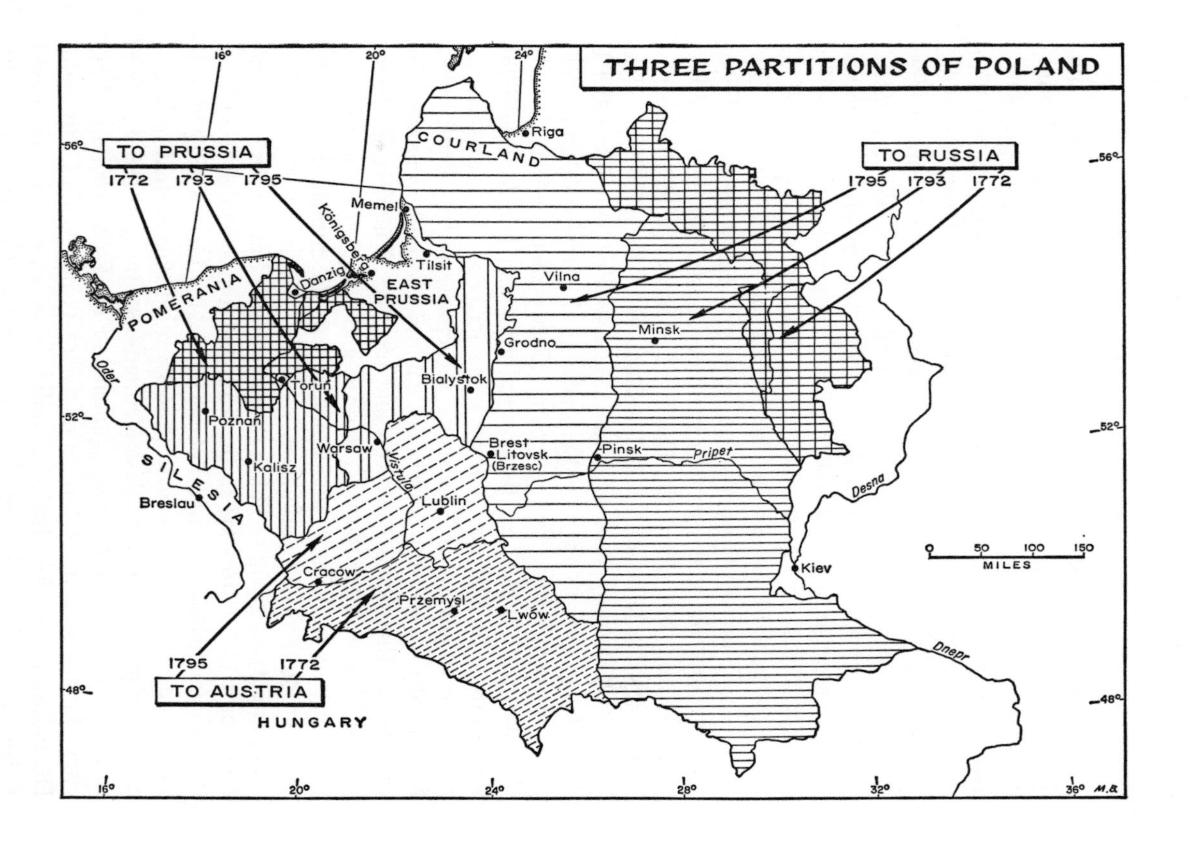
THREE PARTITIONS OF POLAND
TO PRUSSIA
1772
1793
1795
TO RUSSIA
1795
1793
1772
TO AUSTRIA
1795
1772
COURLAND
POMERANIA
EAST PRUSSIA
SILESIA
HUNGARY
Riga
Memel
Königsberg
Tilsit
Danzig
Vilna
Minsk
Grodno
Toruń
Bialystok
Poznań
Warsaw
Brest Litovsk (Brzesc)
Pinsk
Pripet
Kalisz
Vistula
Breslau
Lublin
Cracow
Przemysl
Lwów
Kiev
Desna
Dnepr
Oder
0
50
100
150
MILES
56°
52°
48°
16°
20°
24°
28°
32°
36°
M.Ə.

Poland's eclipse, however, seemed only short-lived. She had gone down in a Europe shaken by revolution, and it could be hoped that the same revolutionary era would help toward her reemergence. Legions of Polish refugees fought in the armies of the young Napoleon as early as 1797, and ten years later, at the Peace of Tilsit, the French emperor finally fulfilled, in a rather grudging way, the dream of those fighters: he established a Polish state ruled by Poles, with a constitution that retained some elements of the constitution of 1791, but was more progressive in social and economic matters though less democratic politically. It was a rather small state, containing mainly the territories gained by Prussia in the Second and Third Partitions, and after the Franco-Austrian War of 1809 also the Austrian gains of 1795, but not the major eastern parts of Galicia. Nor was the state called Poland, but rather the Duchy of Warsaw (with the king of Saxony as duke), because a full restoration of the Polish kingdom would have been opposed by Napolean's new ally, Tsar Alexander I. Thus it was only in 1812, at the opening of Napoleon's great campaign against Russia, that an extraordinary diet in Warsaw proclaimed the restitution of the Polish-Lithuanian kingdom with the borders of 1772. The Polish army, some 100,000 men strong, largely under the command of Stanisław's II nephew Joseph Poniatowski, fought with the greatest bravery but could do nothing to prevent the catastrophe that befell Napoleon and his allies. The decision about Poland's future, after the wars of 1813 and 1814, now was made by the Congress of Vienna, and among them the former partitioning powers wielded decisive influence.

An important group of Polish magnates, with the famous "Family" (the house of Czartoryski) in the lead, had long regarded the tsar as the only one who could save Poland by making himself king of a restored, autonomous, and constitutionally ruled Poland, tied to Russia merely by personal union. Alexander had been more or less won over to the idea by the persuasive arguments of his Polish friend and adviser—for a time even his foreign minister—Prince Adam Czartoryski. He and his friends felt that even under a Russian ruler a truly united Poland would be able to regain and retain her strength as a nation. Prussia was half ready to accept this solution provided that she was compensated by the annexation of Saxony, but Austria and Britain opposed it, feeling that this would mean too much gain for Russia and a dangerous change in the European balance of power.

The final compromise implied nothing less than a Fourth Partition. Austria, in the main, retained what she had gained in the First Partition, Prussia received more than that; in addition to West Prussia she also gained the western part of what she had received in 1793, the so-called Grand Duchy of Posen (Poznań). Of the remaining ethnically Polish territories, most fell to Russia, albeit under the name of Kingdom of Poland, with Alexander as king and (at first) a Polish general as viceroy. Polish hopes that at least those territories that Russia had taken in 1795 would be restored to the "Kingdom" were soon disappointed. Poland, indeed, entered those hundred years—in which the Vienna-created Concert of Europe dominated the world—as a badly split nation. Yet much would now depend, even for the development of Austrian and Prussian Poland, upon the degree to which Alexander's kingdom, often called Congress-Poland, would retain that autonomy solemnly promised to her.

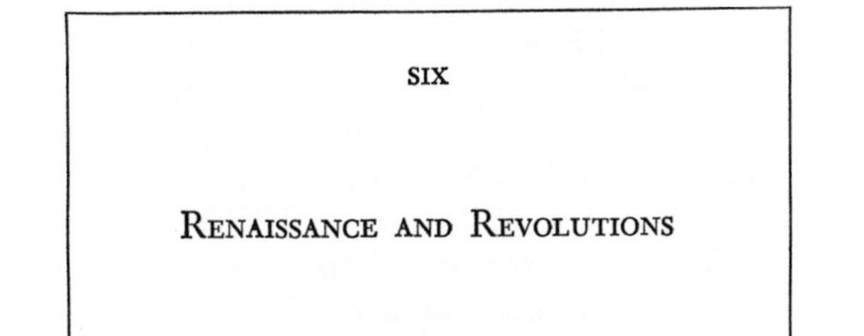

SIX

Renaissance and Revolutions

When, in the period from 1772 to 1815, Poland underwent the tragic series of partitions, modern nationalism had developed to the point at which there was no longer any real danger of the Polish people disappearing as a national body, even though national consciousness was fully alive only among the gentry. In the case of Czechs and Slovaks this was, at the turn from the eighteenth to the nineteenth century, not quite so clear. True, the Hapsburg rulers had never ceased to call themselves kings of Bohemia, had indeed never failed to have themselves crowned with the ancient Crown of St. Wenceslas. But Prague, Bohemia's old capital and prominent seat of Czech culture, national consciousness, and political expression, had, in the mid-eighteenth century, the aspect of a German city. There was, it is true, always a Czech-speaking class of small traders, craftsmen, and workers, but the upper middle class had become largely Germanized. If, among the upper layers of society, there was any remainder of Czech national feelings it could more readily be found among some members of the high nobility, whose sense of history made them aware of the role which their ancestors had played in the Czech state and society of bygone ages. Some of these men vigorously favored and supported the renaissance of Czech national consciousness that began in the Josephinian period. This was, at first, a purely cultural movement.

CZECH CULTURE AND NATIONALISM

To some extent Czech nationalism expressed itself in the form of historiography, for example, in the publications of the Piarist G. Dobner, the Jesuit F. Pubička, and the still more patriotic F. M. Pelcl. These men, writing throughout the second half of the eighteenth century, still used, besides Latin, mostly German, but Pelcl was, in 1792, appointed Professor of the Czech Language at the University of Prague. The attention paid to cultural matters had, already under Joseph II, received an important boost by the founding, in 1784, of the Royal Bohemian Society of Sciences. In 1799 followed an Academy of Fine Arts in Prague, and in 1818 the Bohemian Museum Society, probably the most important of these institutions, not only because of the establishment of a national museum in Prague but even more so because of the publication, beginning soon after, of the great scientific journal, the *Časopis českého musea*, appearing for some time in two editions, a German and a Czech one. Among the early figures of the Czech renaissance perhaps the greatest was Abbé J. Dobrovský (1753-1829) who laid the foundations for critical and scientific studies not only in the history and structure of Czech but of all Slavic languages and who can be considered as the true founder of Slavonic studies everywhere, including even Russian studies and research in the development of Church Slavonic. Of not much less importance was J. Jungmann, author of a great history of Czech literature and of a voluminous dictionary of Czech which became basic in its effects on the development of the language. One of Dobrovský's leading disciples was the philosopher Bernhard Bolzano (1781-1848), like Dobrovský a Catholic priest who became a liberal. It is of special significance that this great movement of awakening was by no means limited to Czechs, but included a number of Slovak thinkers, writers, and teachers. Quite a few of these were Protestants, some of whom had studied at the universities of Jena and Halle. Others were Catholics, often educated at the Catholic-Latin University of Trnava in Slovakia. Among the former were the poet Jan Kollár, famous for his great poem *Slava's Daughter*, written in Czech somewhat after the model of Dante's *Divine Comedy*, and Pavel Josef Šafařík, author of the Czech-written work *Slav Antiquities*, which laid the ground for the development of a cultural Pan-Slavism which was fated, eventually, also to have considerable impact on political trends. But besides the use of Czech as a written language, Slovak forms claimed recognition. As early as 1787 the Catholic Priest A. Bernolák, followed by Jan Holly (both Trnava-educated) developed a written Slovak language using the dialect spoken in Western Slovakia. This was, in the 1830s, replaced by another form, based on a Central Slovak dialect, and developed by L'udevit Štúr (1815-56), which soon became the standard Slovak used to this day. Though its differences from Czech are somewhat more obvious than were those of Bernolák's, the two languages are still so close that the difference as such does not form any barrier for easy mutual understanding in linguistic terms. And Štúr himself favored the closest cooperation, within the Hapsburg monarchy, of Slovaks and Czechs, an attitude held by many leading personalities on both sides.

It was, however, a historian who had the most lasting influence upon the further development of Czechoslovak history. František Palacký descended from an old Moravian family belonging to the Unity of Brethren which had, after Joseph's II edict of toleration, accepted Lutheranism. Educated in the Protestant Lyceum (College) of Bratislava he soon came under the influence of Dobrovský, who introduced him to some patriotic magnates, especially to the Counts of Sternberg, in whose archives he gained much insight into the older history of Bohemia. His appointment as official historiographer of the Kingdom of Bohemia enabled him to write (in Czech as well as in German) his monumental *History of the Czech Nation in Bohemia and Moravia.* In it he established his special understanding and interpretation of the history of his nation; it was dominated by a romantic, idealistic nationalism which attributed to the Czech people, especially in its great age of Hussite struggle, a role of humanist leadership that made it possible for contemporary Czechs to look with intense pride upon their glorious past and to believe again in a future, at least—as Palacký thought for some time—a national future within the framework of a truly supranational Hapsburg empire. It is difficult to overestimate the effect that his writings had on the awakening Czech middle class and intelligentsia. Palacký became, for some decades, the most prominent and most unreservedly recognized intellectual as well as political leader for the Czechs in Bohemia and Moravia. His role was especially conspicuous when the waves of the great revolution of 1848 reached and crossed Bohemia's borders. This revolution, in which the middle class of the cities began to play the leading part, saw in Bohemia and Moravia, and especially in Prague, for a short time the liberals among both Czechs and Germans struggling to get rid of the most oppressive elements of Hapsburg reaction. In Prague, on March 11, a large assembly in the St. Wenceslas Baths had put its emphasis on political demands—freedom of the press, the emancipation of the peasantry, a strenghened legislative for the Kingdom of Bohemia—and equality of languages. Fulfillment of these demands was promised by Emperor Ferdinand in early April, but soon after this the announcement of a rather centralistic constitution for the whole empire seemed to contradict those promises, a fact that created grave doubts among the Czechs. Their leader Palacký meantime refused the invitation of the *Vorparlament* of Frankfurt to join the German patriots in their effort to create a unified and liberal German Reich. The Czechs, he said, had never been and would never be Germans. Their proper place, at this time, was within a Hapsburg empire—based on the free association of nations and resisting with equal vigor all attempts at Pan-Germanism, Pan-Russianism, or Pan-Magyarism. "If Austria" he said, "did not exist it would be necessary to create her, in the interests of Europe and of humanity itself." Unfortunately, the sort of Austria that Palacký envisaged did not exist, and all later endeavors to create it ended in failure. Attempts by Czech moderates, headed by Count Leo Thun, to establish in Prague a government loyal to the dynasty but with true autonomy for Bohemia miscarried, and while the emperor fled from Vienna to Innsbruck, Palacký and his friends, in answer to Frankfurt, and partly following ideas presented by Štúr, called to Prague a great congress of the Slavs of the monarchy, with guests from other Slav countries. The best known, and almost only, Russian present was the famous exiled anarchist Michael Bakunin. The congress was largely under Czech and Slovak leadership. Šafařík gave the opening address, Palacký was chairman, and the Slovak voice came through in ringing tones from L'udevit Štúr, Michael Hodža, and Joseph Miloslav Hurban. The last two were Lutheran pastors who in Hungary had, in vain, tried to stem the tide of a frenzied Magyar chauvinism in favor of justice for the Slav nationalities. Croats and Serbs were also strongly represented, the Serbs by their great leader Vuk Karadžič, and the Slovenes by their leading poet, Stanko Vraz. The Poles, on the other hand, though fairly represented, were reluctant to commit themselves, as they felt themselves drawn to the Magyars, whose struggle for a Hungarian republic was soon to be helped by Polish military leaders.

The Congress refused to accept Bakunin's radical demands for the complete abolition of the Austrian state and instead backed Palacký's program. But before it could be fully spelled out, the revolution erupted again in the so-called Whitsuntide riots. They were bloodily suppressed by the Austrian military commander, Prince Windischgrätz, who soon afterwards performed the same service during the counterrevolution in Vienna.

Meantime, the revolution in Hungary had taken a strange turn. While demanding—for the Magyar gentry as the true representatives of Hungary—full freedom from Hapsburg oppression, the Magyar leaders, especially Louis Kossuth—incidentally, a man of Slovak origin—denied all rights of free development to the non-Magyar nations of Hungary, who represented more than half of the population. The Slovaks reacted vigorously, and on May 10, at an assembly held at Liptovský Svätý Mikuláš, they presented a basic national program demanding the free use of the Slovak language in public and before courts, the establishment of a Slovak school system from primary schools up to the university level, and separate diets for each nationality of the monarchy, that is also for Slovakia; it did not, however, intend to destroy the old coherence of the Crown of St. Stephen. When these demands were rejected by the Magyar leaders, the Slovaks went one step further, and in the fall of 1848, supporting the Austrian government when it sent the Croatian general Jelačić against Hungary, came out openly for close cooperation between Slovaks and Czechs. This development influenced also Palacký's further action.

The constituent *Reichstag* for the Austrian lands, which had meantime been called to Vienna, was moved to the small Moravian town of Kroměříž (Kremsier) in November. There, through January and February 1849, a new constitution for the monarchy was drafted and passed, largely under Palacký's spiritual leadership, by the constitutional committee. Based on the principle of equality of all nationalities, the Hapsburg Empire was to be organized in a federal union in which Czechs and Slovaks, Poles and Ruthenians, Slovenes and Croatians and Serbs would have their states or autonomous provinces just as Germans, Magyars, Italians, and Rumanians. It was the fairest and most imaginative plan for reform as yet developed for the Hapsburg Empire. But only three days after the committee had accepted it and before it could even be submitted to the plenum, the *Reichstag* was dissolved by the young Emperor Francis Joseph, who had succeeded his uncle Ferdinand upon the latter's abdication. After a short experiment with an imposed constitution, the empire reverted, under the absolutist regime of Alexander Bach, to a state hardly better than it had been at Metternich's time. The Revolution of 1848 had been a pitiful failure for Bohemia, as it had been for most of Central Europe, and in the following years the hopes for a peaceful, constructive cooperation of Czechs and Germans in Bohemia and Moravia were vanishing fast.

DISMEMBERED POLAND AND ÉMIGRÉ POLES

For Poland, too, the years after 1815 were a period of repeated bitter disappointments. In Russian-held Congress-Poland, there seemed at first to be some hope for the continuation of a high degree of national autonomy under Tsar Alexander. His brother Constantine Pavlovich, commander in chief of the separate Polish army, who as such wielded great power, and who was married to a Polish noblewoman, had genuine sympathy for the country and its people and before long identified himself largely with Polish interests. But he was not an able administrator, nor were the reactionary Polish aristocrats who governed the kingdom. Even though Finance Minister Lubecki was an able man, the ministry as a whole was not capable of stemming the steady deterioration of the economic situation. This led to great dissatisfaction among the peasantry and other parts of the population. The King-Emperor listened less and less to the advice of Adam Czartoryski, the actual author of the scheme of Russo-Polish personal union, and more to the Russian High Commissioner (or tsarist ambassador) to the kingdom, Count Novosiltsov. Things grew far worse, however, in spite of some economic improvement during the 1820s, when in 1825 Alexander died and his youngest brother Nicholas followed him. He suspected, surely not quite wrongly, that the Decembrist revolution which had broken out at the moment of his succession had had its supporters in Poland and Lithuania, and tried, unsuccessfully, to force a supreme court appointed by the Senate to sentence arrested Polish patriots. But the real explosion came only in November 1830, when reports circulated that Nicholas intended to use Polish troops to suppress the French July revolution. The rebellion was started by young cadets, but soon, despite attempts by some elder statesmen as well as by Grand Duke Constantine to reach some compromise by negotiations, it became a real and widespread revolution against the tsar, who was deposed as king of Poland. The struggle took the forms of a fairly prolonged war, but as the Poles did not receive any help from other countries, Russian numerical strength decided the issue. In September 1831 the Russian general Paskevich conquered Warsaw, and one month later most of the remaining Polish forces crossed the Prussian borders, many of them eventually reaching the sanctuary of French soil, where a very active community of Polish émigrés began the long and frustrating task of mobilizing European public opinion in favor of the restitution of a free Poland.

Actually, the situation of the Poles in their homelands, far from improving, grew steadily worse. In Prussia as well as in Austria the monarchical regimes reacted by restricting the limited freedoms of the Polish people, and especially in Congress-Poland an oppressive military occupation headed by Paskevich operated with extreme severity. Alexander's constitution was replaced by an "organic statute" abolishing the Polish army and all forms of representation for the people. Institutions of higher learnings, especially the universities in Vilna and Warsaw, were closed. The leaders of the revolution who had not been able to escape felt the revenge of the victor.

Under these circumstances Polish hopes to profit from the next great revolutionary wave were not fulfilled. In Cracow and Galicia a prelude to 1848—an insurrection that broke out in 1846—was easily suppressed by the Austrian authorities, who made full use of the antagonism existing between gentry and peasants, thus causing considerable loss of life among the gentry. This was one of the causes that in 1848 made a Polish national revolution in Austrian Poland a faint hope to begin with.

Things were different, however, in Prussian Poland. The mood prevailing in many parts of Germany during the early phases of the revolution seemed highly favorable to the Poles who were often considered as potential allies. Beside the general emotions of international friendship that the "Spring of Nations" had evoked, the German and especially the Prussian liberals were worried that the ominous rumblings coming from St. Petersburg might actually turn into open intervention on the part of Tsar Nicholas I. Already in the heady days of March, in Berlin, the Polish General Mierosławski had been freed from prison (having been detained after an attempted rebellion in 1846) and, after much celebration, allowed to go to Poznania. During the short term of office of the strongly Polonophile Count Arnim-Boitzenburg, King Frederick William IV approved of a scheme giving Poznania an autonomy almost amounting to independence, with her own army and administration, as a step toward Polish reunification. The Prussian authorities permitted the formation of a Polish National Committee, which also began to organize military forces. But there was no clear policy on either side, and old antagonisms were bound to make themselves felt. Attempts at a compromise by the Polonophile General Willisen, who had been sent to Poznania as royal commissioner, soon foundered in the outbreak of mutual distrust and discrimination. Eventually the Prussian government suppressed the movement of liberation by military means, and even considered splitting Poznania into two parts, an eastern one to remain Polish, and possibly to be ceded to Russia, and a western one from which all Poles would be evicted toward the east. This plan was finally rejected by the Prussian Parliament, and all hopes for Polish liberation through Prussian cooperation had been shattered. The immediate harvest of the 1848 revolution for the Polish people was a bad one in Prussia and, at least for most of the 1850s, also in Austria.

Only in Russian-ruled Congress-Poland there seemed, for a short while, some hope for an improvement of conditions when, after the loss of the Crimean War and the death of Tsar Nicholas I, his successor, Alexander II, tried a certain measure of liberalization for the kingdom. The economic pulse of the country was quickened by the removal of the customs barrier between Poland and Russia, a step which helped the growth of Polish industries and began to make Łódź the "Manchester of the East." The University of Warsaw, closed under Nicholas, was reopened. More influence was given to Poles in the administration. Alexander even looked for a man who would play the role which Prince Adam Czartoryski, who died in Paris, an embittered leader of the emigration, in 1861, had played to his uncle Alexander I. He found him in Count Alexander Wielopolski, a genuine patriot who hoped to gain, by cooperation, a maximum of autonomy within the tsarist empire. But he found little support among the majority of the Polish upper and middle classes, who looked at any compromise with the Russians as a betrayal of the principles of Polish national freedom. Offers of autonomy presented to the Poles in the tsar's name by the viceroy, Grand Duke Constantine Nikolayevich, were answered by an ultimatum delivered to the viceroy by the Polish nobility organized in the so-called Agricultural Society, demanding full freedom not only for Poland but also Lithuania and Ruthenia. Eventually, Wielopolski attempted to bring the issue into the open and thereby defeat it, by having the youth of the cities called up to army service. But he played with fire. As a result of his step, on January 22, 1863, a revolution broke out which, limited at first, soon became nationwide. But because of the poor means at its disposal, taking mainly the form of guerrilla warfare, and the overwhelming power of the Russian armed forces, it never had the slightest chance of success. Western attempts to influence the Russian government by diplomatic pressure only led to stricter suppression, supported also by the Prussian government under Bismarck through the so-called Alvensleben Convention. The revolution of 1863, thus, resulted merely in a further painful diminution of Polish freedom. Even the shadows of Polish statehood, even the name of an autonomous political existence, were now wiped out, and what had been called the Kingdom of Poland became the Vistula Provinces of the tsar's empire. Russification was now the goal of the government, first, most thoroughly and not unsuccessfully, in the Lithuanian, Byelorussian, and Ukrainian territories that had shown the strong remaining influence of Polish traditions and feelings by their participation (still very strong in 1831) in the Polish revolutions. But even in ethnically purely Polish regions little was left of Polish education, and the process of Russification in the former Kingdom of Poland found a close parallel in an equally systematic policy of Germanization in Posen and West Prussia, especially exacerbated in the '70s by Bismarck's *Kulturkampf*. Indeed, it would have been hard for Polish culture to survive if it had not been for the strength of the Polish spirit among the refugees.

In a way the Polish emigration, which contained the very essence of the Polish spirit in the decades following 1831, was a later parallel to the Czech emigration that had taken place after 1620. But the "Great Emigration" of the Poles expressed itself most vividly in

Polish romanticism. Among the artists representative of this romantic Poland no other is as well known as the composer Frederick Chopin who, even before the rising of 1831, had left Warsaw for France and never returned. His strongly national musical form was continued by lesser heirs, in the works of Moniuszko and Wieniawski. In literature probably the greatest of the Romantics of this era was the poet Adam Mickiewicz (1798-1855), whose position in Poland had already been undermined by his contacts with the Decembrists, who joined the Parisian community of Polish émigrés and died in 1855 during his attempt to organize Polish legions for participation in the Crimean War. Of his rich production the historic epic *Konrad Wallenrod* and above all the great idyllic verse novel *Pan Tadeusz* are dominant Polish classics to this day, and the latter achieved, through translations, a considerable measure of international fame. With Mickiewicz the "Polish Byron," Julius Słowacki (1809-49), and the most political of Polish refugee-poets, Zygmunt Krasiński (1812-59), formed a trio that was to dominate Polish literary values as well as some Polish political thoughts and hopes for a long time to come. Encouraging, as in Bohemia, was also the systematic study of Poland's great past. It was then that Poland's greatest historian, Joachim Lelewel (1786-1861), wrote his monumental works on Polish history as well as his remarkably original studies in the fields of medieval geography and numismatics. He was, however, just as his younger Czech contemporary Palacký, deeply interested in the shaping of the world of his time, and while he could not, like Palacký, be a political leader at home, he worked hard for the formation of a Polish liberal and democratic spirit. Yet, much though the émigrés contributed to the salvation and the flourishing of Polish culture in a period of political darkness and near despair, the more permanent and basic work had still to be done in the Polish lands themselves.

MATURING NATIONS—THEIR WORK AND STRUGGLE

During the later nineteenth century the West Slav nations were still in a position where their freedom of development depended to a considerable extent upon the policy of the foreign governments under whose rule they were forced to live. In Russian Poland nothing happened during the decades following 1863 that to any extent alleviated the fate of the Polish people. Beside the systematic destruction of Polish education, a veritable war was conducted against the Catholic church in Poland, and even more fanatically against the Uniat church which, in previous times, had played some role in tying Byelorussians and Ukrainians in the former Grand Duchy of Lithuania more firmly to the Polish-Lithuanian state. While the Tsarist depolonization policy in those eastern regions was not quite unsuccessful, the attack on the church in Poland only served to strengthen Catholicism among the majority of the people.

The same was true, in a similar way, of the Poles of Germany. During the *Kulturkampf* Bismarck went so far as to have the Archbishop of Gniezno-Poznań, the very moderate later Cardinal Ledóchowski, as well as other bishops imprisoned when they resisted the substitution of German for Polish in the religious instruction of Polish children. In view of the hopelessness, for the time being, to make either in Russian or in Prussian Poland any gains toward autonomy, let alone independence, the mood in large parts of the Polish middle class changed from the long-prevailing attitude of all-out fight, without counting the odds, against the partitioning powers to that of a more pragmatic attitude aimed at assuring the survival and, if possible, the economic strengthening of the Polish people. It was called "organic work," and in both countries, Russia and Germany, it had in the long run, and in spite of occasional setbacks, a measure of success. In Russian Poland there could, of course, never be any question of a really effective denationalization or Russification of the Polish population. Brutal as the tsarist regime was, it did not have the audacity, nor could it quite afford, in view of an active public opinion in Western Europe, to consider seriously what the Nazis more than considered during World War II—genocidal extermination of the Poles in the heartland of their ancient state. In Germany, on the other hand, leading statesmen, from Bismarck to Bülow, were at this time worried about the large and fast growing Polish population in Poznania, West Prussia, and Upper Silesia, and about the fact that this population also gained economic strength, in rural areas as well as in the cities, through systematic cooperative action. Against it the German government tried to mobilize quite enormous capital investments with the goal of buying up Polish-owned estates and settling them with German farmers. This measure was accompanied, in 1886, by the expulsion of many thousands of

Poles who had lived, some of them for decades, in East Germany but had no German citizenship. All those measures had some passing effects, but in the long run merely made the Polish people, inside as well as outside the Reich, consider imperial Germany to be just as dangerous an enemy as tsarist Russia.

The Hapsburg Empire remained as the only one of the partitioning powers where Poles could live in some degree of freedom. This, in the last decades of the century, was growing in the same measure in which its last traces had been removed elsewhere. In Austria, of course, the Poles had the original advantage of not being a relatively small part of the population faced by a single huge national majority. The Austrian Poles were also better off, in the political struggle for influence inside the empire, than the Czechs. In Galicia their proportional strength was not so different from that of the Czechs in Bohemia, Moravia and "Austrian Silesia," yet the Czechs had to deal with a German population which, after the dream of cooperation under the heading "Böhmischer Landespatriotismus" had been dispelled by the developments of 1848-49, were determined to hold their position as the dominant nation in the countries of the Crown of St. Wenceslas and not to give anything like equality to the Czechs, whom they considered as culturally, and frequently even "racially," inferior. The situation of the Poles was better. In Galicia the "other nation" was the Ukrainians, and there it was the Poles who looked down on their less developed Slavic brothers. It was characteristic that the capital of Galicia, Lwów (Lemberg), was mainly a Polish city, whereas the surrounding countryside—as well as most of Eastern Galicia—was predominantly Ukrainian. In Poland's former capital, Cracow, and after 1867 in Lwów, there were universities, indeed, the only Polish universities in existence which, in the late nineteenth century, served not only the Polish people under Hapsburg rule but also large numbers of Poles from the territories under Russian and German rule. Without them it would have been infinitely more difficult to maintain and develop further a strong and up-to-date Polish civilization.

Of the many different nations living in the Hapsburg Empire the Poles were better equipped to make use of the struggle which all the Austrian Slavs waged with renewed vigor after 1848, especially when, with the demise of the centralist absolutism of the Bach regime, all further attempts at strengthening the Ukrainians against the Poles were for the time being given up. Much of the work for Polish self-government was done by a Polish grandee for whom the Emperor Francis Joseph had strong personal sympathies, Count Agenor Gołuchowski, who, after a period as governor of Galicia, was in 1859 appointed minister of the interior and a year later prime minister of the empire. As such he tried, through the so-called October Diploma of 1860, to revive some of the ideas of the Kroměříž diet for a federal reorganization of the empire. But much as in 1849 so in 1860 the scheme was buried after less than two months and Gołuchowski's cabinet had to give place to a more centralist one led by Schmerling, to the severe disappointment of both Poles and Czechs who, in June 1861, withdrew from the Vienna parliament. When Austria's conflict with Prussia became critical the emperor and his advisers looked for new ways of strengthening the monarchy. It was obvious that complete centralization against the wishes of all nations except the Germans could not work. Francis Joseph might at this stage have taken the course hoped for by the Slavic nations, but instead he decided to restore merely the position of Hungary, thereby thwarting, for a long time, all hopes (nourished by Palacký and his disciples) for a reorganization uniting Czechs and Slovaks.

Indeed, the *Ausgleich*, and the dualistic system created by it, destroyed not only a Czech-Slovak combination but also the chance for a restoration of a truly autonomous state comprising, within the Hapsburg Empire, the three lands of the Crown of St. Wenceslas. Whenever, in the following years, negotiations between the crown and the Czechs gave the impression that the Czech demand for "state rights" might lead to something concrete, the sharp reaction of Hungarians and Germans blocked any progress. The Czechs, however, who, under the leadership of Palacký's son-in-law Ladislav Rieger, fought with rigid consistency just for this state right, continued to boycott the parliament (*Reichsrat*) in Vienna and, at times, even the Bohemian diet, leaving the field entirely to the Germans. It was a policy followed by Rieger and his party until, in 1879, the appointment of Count Eduard Taaffe, himself a Bohemian magnate of Irish descent, gave the Czechs a strong chance to influence the political development in their favor. A newly rising party, the "Young Czechs," led by the two brothers Grégr and later by Karel

Kramář, gave up the barren policy of abstention. From now on the Czechs began to play an important role in the *Reichsrat*, and together with the Poles, who had dropped the policy of abstention in 1873, and the Christian Social Party they formed the coalition called "Iron ring" which made Taaffe's the longest-lived government (1879-94) which *Cisleithania* (the non-Hungarian part of the empire) enjoyed throughout the existence of the dual monarchy. The presence of a prominent Pole, the gifted Minister of Finance Dunajewski, and the competent Czech Minister of Justice A. Pražák, symbolized progress which, while far from satisfying the Czechs, still contributed toward strengthening their position in the political arena of the monarchy. There was a better representation of Czechs in the Bohemian diet. But, for the Czech mind, of at least equal importance was the first in a series of language decrees, ordering, among other things, all offices in the Bohemian crown lands to answer all communications in the language in which they were received. The decree met with severe criticism from the Germans, since most German civil servants had so far disdained learning Czech. In the longer run it improved the opportunities for educated Czechs—most of whom were fully bilingual—to obtain administrative positions.

Education, especially higher education, in Czech was considerably improved when in 1882 the University of Prague, which, after its Latin past, had been Germanized in the eighteenth century, was divided into two independent institutions, one Czech, one German. Together with the new National Theater which, having opened in 1881, almost immediately burned down and was rebuilt by the pennies of the people, the Czech University, vigorously assuming the great traditions of the ancient Carolina, changed the whole aspect of Czech cultural and intellectual status and development and also helped not a little in the rapid proliferation of a sound secondary school system. It also strengthened Czech ideological influence in other parts of the Hapsburg Empire, among Slovenes, Croats, and Serbs, but above all among Slovaks many of whom now enrolled as students in Prague.

This small nation's chances even for a secondary education in their own language had been completely destroyed when in 1875, in the course of the stepped-up Magyarization drive, the last of those high schools had been forcibly closed which the Slovaks, without any state support, had developed out of their own meager resources. It was not only in the field of education that the Slovaks were thrown back and reduced to utter impotence at the very time when the Czech nation, for all the resistance encountered from German nationalists, steadily gained strength. What little there was of a Slovak press could only work under the most severe restrictions. A totally distorting voting procedure gave, around the turn of the century, more than two million Slovaks a representation in Parliament of at best seven, and more frequently two, one, or no deputies. As before in the early awakening of Slovak national consciousness Protestant (Lutheran) groups frequently displayed a stronger initiative and exerted a proportionately greater influence than the Catholic majority of the nation.

Among the Protestants was, above all, Milan Hodža, a man who was to play an important role later. The strongest Catholic leader was the Ružomberok priest Andrew Hlinka, who became internationally well known when his attempt to have a Slovak chapel consecrated at the village of Černova led to a massacre of quietly demonstrating Slovak peasants by Magyar police. Hlinka and his friends were imprisoned, as was also Hodža. The last years before World War I made it appear truly doubtful how long the Slovak nation would be able to withstand the terrific pressure, and tens of thousands sought a better life by emigrating to America.

Meanwhile, in the Austrian half of the monarchy, parliamentary parties developed strongly among Czechs as well as Poles. As the lands of the Crown of St. Wenceslas and, to a lesser extent, Galicia underwent a strong industrialization and more and more peasants turned into workers, socialism was bound to develop in both nations. In Bohemia there arose, besides a Marxian social democratic party founded in 1878, a "nationalist socialist" party which, in addition to workers, could also attract a not insignificant number of middle-class people. Somewhat to the right of them stood the Catholic "People's Party," while the Young Czechs, slowly drifting toward the right, eventually turned into the party called National Democrats. Their greatest leader was Karel Kramář, a cultured grand seigneur, a powerful personality and a consistent representative of Pan-Slavism. In the years prior to 1914 he worked for a strengthening of all Slavic elements within the Hapsburg monarchy, whose close alliance with Germany he deplored and attacked. When in 1895 the Polish magnate Count Casimir Badeni became prime minister and began to resume the policy of Gołuchowski and Taaffe, Kramář and his friend J. Kaizl conducted negotiations that resulted in a new series of language decrees strengthening the Slavs and, at the same time, deeply annoying the Germans. Kaizl, a university professor, became minister of finance, and for a short while, under the chancellorship of Körber, better understanding seemed to open up, with the crown favoring concessions to the Slavs. But, as earlier, the emperor, under German and Magyar pressure, never persisted in this course, and by 1904 the Czech members of the *Reichsrat* were again engaged in bitter fighting with the Germans. Meanwhile, in Prague, a man of singular qualities began to gather around himself a circle of idealistic realists, mainly among the Czech intelligentsia—Thomas G. Masaryk.

This greatest of Czech statesmen of modern times, born in a small Moravian town near the Hungarian—in ethnic terms Slovak—border, was the son of a mixed Czech-Slovak marriage of the simplest social standing but he managed to work his way through schools and universities until, in 1882, he was appointed professor of philosophy at the newly separated Czech University in Prague. His unconditional devotion to truth and justice was proved when he, with some philological helpers, revealed that the famous Dvůr Králové manuscript, supposedly medieval Czech poetry of great beauty, had in fact been forged early in the 19th century by its "discoverer," the gifted writer Václav Hanka; and similarly, when he did veritable detective work in pointing out the barbarous anti-Semitic absurdities and distortions of law in the trial of the young Jewish journeyman Hilsner who was accused of ritual murder of a Christian child. In both cases Masaryk had to face fierce public antagonism but was eventually fully justified before his nation and the world. After an earlier period in the Vienna parliament he founded in 1900 a new party, the Realists, but it never became very strong. Yet he was one of the most influential people in the monarchy, partly because of his intimate contact with other Slavic groups, especially the Croats and Serbs. By 1914 no other Czech enjoyed as much respect inside the Hapsburg monarchy and in the West as well as did Masaryk. Indeed, it is difficult to exaggerate the role that he played during and after World War I.

The same might be said in regard to Poland of Józef Piłsudski.

And just as Masaryk was, for a long time, to have to contend for the role of leadership with Kramář, the head of the National Democrats, so Piłsudski found himself, before long, in disagreement with Roman Dmowski, the leader of a Polish party also called the National Democrats. There were, indeed, some similarities between Kramář and Dmowski. Both believed that for all Slavs, even for the Poles, Russian leadership was needed, though tsarist oppression in Russian Poland made this stand much more difficult. Dmowski, following the traditions of Czartoryski (prior to 1830) and Wielopolski, after the 1905 revolution in Russia and the creation of a parliament, the Duma, for the whole tsarist empire, tried to lead the National Democratic party in a way which would strengthen chances of a Polish-Russian understanding. This, also, was the policy he explained when participating, on Kramář's invitation, at another great Slavic Congress held in Prague in July 1908.

Piłsudski, on the other hand, could see hardly any possibilities of an understanding with tsarist Russia. Coming from the region of Vilna, he absorbed and developed to real strength that Polish socialism which had had its beginnings among the émigrés in France, England, and Switzerland and which became an underground movement in Congress Poland in the 1880s. Five years in Siberia (1887-92) helped to make him an irreconcilable enemy of Russia. After a long and fierce political struggle, partly waged by means of a clandestine revolutionary newspaper, the *Robotnik*, Piłsudski was in 1900 arrested again but soon after escaped to Austria. There he began, during the early years of the twentieth century, a feverish activity, especially among Polish students in Galicia, preparing them for the possibility of war and of military action against Russia. The Austrian authorities knew of it but did not interfere in his work. When war came in August 1914 he was probably the only one of the important leaders of the West Slav nations who was thoroughly prepared for it.

In this short survey of the development of the West Slav nations in the five decades after 1863 a word must still be said about their cultural development. The great wave of romanticism that dominated Polish literature in the first half of the century gave way, after 1863, to the rise of realist tendencies, which dominated especially the development of the novel. Its most prominent representatives tended to combine works of social significance with the writing of historical novels. This was true for Bolesław Prus (1847-1912) and even more for his contemporary Henryk Sienkiewicz (1846-1916), internationally famous for his *Quo Vadis* which got him, as the first Polish writer, the Nobel prize. Possibly Władysław Reymont (1868-1925), the second Pole thus marked for distinction, achieved an even more lasting fame by his huge work *The Peasants*, which combines the description of the everyday life of the Polish peasantry throughout the year with a deeper penetration into the mysteries of the human soul. The man who, conceivably, might have become the greatest of Polish writers in the late nineteenth and early twentieth centuries never published his work in his mother language. Teodor Józef Korzeniowski (1857-1924), a young emigrant who went to sea on British ships, became one of the most powerful writers of the English language. It was only during World War I that, in speaking up for the restoration of his homeland, Joseph Conrad turned back to Polish issues and problems.

In the field of music, the romantic tradition, carried over from Chopin by Moniuszko and Wieniawski, was still maintained into the twentieth century by Karol Szymanowski (1883-1937), who had, by the outbreak of the war, already achieved general recognition as a highly gifted and unusually versatile composer. The dominant figure of Poland's musical life at the beginning of the present century, however, was a superb performer first and a composer only to a lesser degree—Ignace Paderewski had impressed the western world to such an extent that he was eventually able to play a role as one of the leaders of the Polish nation.

Music surely was the art in which the Czechs excelled more than in any other. Already in the early second half of the eighteenth century Czech composers—especially such men as J. V. Stamitz, F. X. Richter, and J. A. Benda, had composed fine music and had prominently contributed to the development of the so-called school of Mannheim, which was to have considerable influence on Mozart. This was true also, during the same period, of the first great Czech operatic composer, Josef Mysliveček. Mozart himself entertained close ties with Prague, where he felt to be better understood than in Vienna and where he presented, for the first time, his *Don Giovanni.* But the highest flowering was achieved by Czech music only in the second half of the nineteenth century. At this time the nation produced three real giants, each only about half a generation removed from the other, a triad which, together with some lesser lights, put the Czechs as a musical nation on a level that, if not in quantity, was surely in quality comparable with the greatest creations of nineteenth-century music anywhere in the world.

The first of the three, Bedřich Smetana (1824-84) was perhaps the most important of the European composers of national music based on the folk songs and dances of his people. But while this characterized both his most famous opera, the exhilarating *Bartered Bride*, and his great symphonic cycle *My Fatherland*, all his compositions—operas, orchestral music, and chamber music—grew far above any such label to a level in which rich melodic beauty is matched by structural greatness. He shared Beethoven's bitter fate of the early and complete loss of his hearing, and though he still, even then, managed to write some important operatic music he ended, under this terrific pressure, in insanity. A happier fate—and more recognition—was granted to Antonín Dvořák (1841-1901), whose great symphonic music gave him early international fame, especially in America, where he composed, during a prolonged stay as director of the New York National Conservatory, his highly popular *New World Symphony*. But there was no form of musical expression in which Dvořák was not a master, including operas, among which *Rusalka* is probably the finest. The third of the giants of Czech music, Leoš Janáček, was only 13 years younger than Dvořák but survived him by more than a quarter of a century and did not gain recognition as a composer of the highest rank until the early years of the twentieth century. He came from Moravia and had strong ties with Slovakia and the Slavic world to the east, as expressed most distinctly in his difficult but deep *Glagolitic Mass*. He, too, was at home in many forms of music but was, above all, a creator of great operatic art which was clearly revolutionary when it was written and is to some extent only now fully understood and appreciated.

While Czech music reached, at this time, a higher level than that of Poland, Czech prose literature probably did not equal in rank that of the sister nation. There were some fine writers such as Jan Neruda (1834-91) and Julius Zeyer (1841-1901) followed, a generation later, by the brothers Josef and Karel Čapek and Ivan Olbracht, but the highest literary achievements were probably realized in the field of lyric poetry. The two greatest Czech poets were Otakar Březina (1868-1929), with his powerful mystical verse, and Petr Bezruč (1867-1959), whose *Silesian Songs* had strong social significance and enormous word power. In the lyrical field the Slovaks, too, reached a high level with Svetozár Hurban Vajanský (1847-1916) who, influenced by Russian literature, also wrote strong epic prose, and Pavol Országh Hviezdoslav (1849-1921), whose intense love for the little people of his nation, expressed in a powerful language, made him a symbol of the Slovak resistance to forcible denationalization. Hviezdoslav, a close friend of Masaryk, was read much also in the Czech countries, where, in cultural as well as in political terms, concern with the fate of the Slovaks had continued to grow steadily.

SEVEN

World War I and Independence

The general question of the causes of and the responsibility for World War I cannot concern us in this sketch. But it is obvious that the rulers of the Hapsburg Empire acted with remarkable shortsightedness. In particular, while supposedly defending the monarchy against the attacks of the Slavic Serbs inside and outside her borders, they acted in a way which was bound to destroy whatever loyalty and support the Slavic population, at this moment actually a majority of the total population, had in the past given to the dynasty. Even the measure of respect that the old emperor who had reigned for so long had enjoyed among a good many Slavic "Austro-Hungarians" could not survive in a war that was waged for the destruction of the Serb state and in a life-and-death struggle against Russia.

The view that the war was a crime against the Slavs immediately dominated the public opinion of the great majority of the Czechs as well as the Slovaks. Even though the democratic elements among both had strong reservations toward the tsarist regime, and the earlier romantic Pan-Slavism that had dominated much of Slovak thinking had largely disappeared, both thought of the Serbs as brothers, and in a struggle between imperial Russia and imperial Germany their sympathies were bound to be on the Russian side. The Hapsburg policy, indeed, was felt to have come completely under the influence of the anti-Slavic policy of Germany. From the first day on, not a trace of "Austro-Hungarian patriotism" was felt either by the leaders or the masses of the Czechs or the Slovaks. The attitude of a cautious passive resistance that is characterized with a masterful sarcasm in Jaroslav Hašek's *Good Soldier Švejk* was widespread. And while, especially in periods in which the Central Powers seemed to be irresistibly victorious, even the relatively strong and well organized Czechs could hardly dare openly to take a hostile position against the government, there arose soon a resistance movement both at home (where, for its secretive character, it was soon called "the Mafia"), and abroad, where, as for example in America, Czechs and Slovaks could show without fear on which side their sympathies were.

Only a few daring minds would, at the early stages of the war, go so far as to dream and plan for complete independence. It would, so they saw, only become a real possibility if the war dragged on and gave the Czechs, especially outside the country, the opportunity to influence public opinion among the Entente peoples to the extent that the destruction of the multinational Hapsburg Empire could become an acceptable war aim. However, even if during the early stages of the war this would not seem to be very likely, the majority of the people fervently desired defeat for the Central Powers and thus victory for the Entente. And at a fairly early stage one way of acting for this hoped-for aim was the refusal of Czech and Slovak soldiers to fight, especially to fight against Austria's main enemy Russia. And the next step from this unwillingness to fight was the willingness to join the other side by mass surrender, in the hope eventually to join the Russians in fighting the Austrians and Germans. It was not always an easy thing to do, as the soldiers were in danger of being shot at from the front and the back. Also, once happily in prisoner-of-war camps, the expectation of being allowed to join up again as Czechoslovak forces was fulfilled only in a very small way until the Russian high command, after the terrible losses suffered in 1915 and 1916, was really eager to use every source of trained manpower, including also the fairly numerous people of Czech and Slovak origin living in Russia. In this way a sizable army, called the Czechoslovak Legions, was formed in Russia. It gained some importance after the revolution of early 1917, when the Kerensky government, free from the tsarist prejudices, was glad to use the legions as an autonomous unit under the Russian high command. In this quality, especially during the last Brusilov offensive, the Czechoslovak troops distinguished themselves, for example in the battle of Zborov when, during the first days of July, they broke through an Austrian sector of the Galician front, taking more than 4000 prisoners and much matériel. But this was about the last chance they had to interfere in the east, and the Western allies as well as the Czech émigré leaders soon thought of transferring them to the western front.

The émigré leaders, meantime, had organized themselves into a triumvirate that proved to be extraordinarily effective in fighting the great propaganda battle for the claims of Czechs and Slovaks to national freedom. Their recognized head—recognized as the only possible leader by the Czechs and Slovaks abroad active in the struggle, and also by the French, English, and American friends of their cause, was Thomas G. Masaryk, who had arrived in Paris early in 1915, followed some months later by a disciple, Dr. Edward Beneš, a young sociologist, who for a while had maintained liaison between the Mafia and the émigrés and who proved to be a most gifted, ingenious, and indefatigable worker for the cause. The third member of the triumvirate was Milan Štefánik, a Slovak who had left his homeland in 1902 and had made a brilliant career in France first as an astronomer and, during the war, as an officer—he rose to the rank of brigadier general. He had a romantic mind and was almost the exact opposite of the sober and carefully calculating Beneš. He had less clear goals but had warmth and charm and was as devoted a disciple of Masaryk as was Beneš. He managed to open important French doors to Masaryk, and had also a decisive influence in gaining, after overcoming considerable difficulties, the agreement of Italy. In the end Czechoslovak legions, though not nearly as strong as those in Russia, were engaged in France and in Italy.

The attempt to transfer the strong legions formed in Russia to the western theater of war turned out to be extremely difficult after the conclusion of the Peace of Brest-Litovsk. As the shorter way via Archangelsk was no longer open, the decision was taken to send the troops to Western Europe via the enormously roundabout way of the Transsiberian railroad, Vladivostok, and Japan. But on this attempt, at first approved by the Soviet government, friction arose which led to open conflicts. In their course the legions occupied and held for a while the whole length of the Transsiberian railroad. At one stage the Western governments hoped to use the Czechoslovak troops in support of the Koltchak regime against the Soviets, but this attempt, in spite of some early successes, was short-lived and was given up in favor of quick evacuation in order to strengthen the western front in what appeared to be a decisive period of the war.

The plans for this astonishing enterprise had partly been laid by Masaryk who, in its course, traveled around the world and spent the last months of the war in the United States, where he convinced President Wilson of the justification of the demand for an independent state for Czechs and Slovaks, receiving in the process the full support, and achieving a large measure of mutual understanding, of the Czech and Slovak communities in America. President Wilson's help, indeed, was of crucial importance for the Czechoslovak as well as for the Polish restitution.

POSTWAR POLAND

The situation of the Poles was in one way different from that of Czechs and Slovaks, who could under no circumstances expect to gain from a victory of the Central Powers, and could at least not lose anything if the Entente won. The same could not be said of Poland. Rather there would be reason to fear unpleasant consequences whichever side was winning. A victory of the Entente, with Russia included among the victors, would perhaps result in a Russian annexation of the Polish territories of the Central Powers and thus in a reunion of all Poles under one rule—but it would still be a foreign and might conceivably still be a harsh rule in which especially the Poles of Galicia stood to lose much if not all of that precious freedom they had enjoyed for the last half century. This consideration was bound to be paramount among the most radically Russophobe circles, with Piłsudski at their head. It was logical for members of this group to think that there would at least be a possibility of a movement toward not only reunion but also an autonomy amounting to near independence if, in case of a victory of the Central Powers, the Polish territories were to become part of a federal union under Hapsburg rule. The Polish nation as a whole was considerably larger than either the Austrian Germans or the Magyars, and such a development would increase the total proportion of all Slavic groups within the Hapsburg Empire to an extent where they would be far more dominating than in the past. Thus it could be expected that the status of the Poles within such a combination would be just as strong as that of the Magyars had been under dualism. The whole dualist conception would have to be thoroughly revised in favor of far more influence and independence for each constituent unit.

This hope for an "Austro-Polish" solution of the present crisis was, however, looked at by other groups with extreme distrust and even antagonism. One of the main reasons was that, even if Austria was willing to connect Galicia with a liberated Russian Poland and give this combination a large degree of self-determination, there seemed very little chance for Prussian Poland to be joined to it if the Central Powers won the war. Indeed, for the more or less Russophile groups, headed by Dmowski, Germany was the arch-enemy, and to cooperate with Germany against Russia was madness and betrayal of Poland's future as a Slavic nation. Thus, in the beginning of the war, the gap between the Piłsudski camp and the Dmowski camp widened to what appeared an unbridgeable chasm. In the end it could be partially bridged only by the extraordinary course of the war which no one could have foreseen in 1914—the defeat of all three partitioning powers, of Russia by the Central Powers, and of these afterward by the Western Allies, thus in the end obviating the torturing need of opting for one or the other of the old enemies.

During the early phases of the war, however, it was Piłsudski whose actions made it clear that there was a Polish nation whose will and whose active participation had some significance and could not be neglected. He mobilized his long-trained though poorly armed legions and as early as August 6 crossed the Russian border for the conquest of the town of Kielce. The Austrian government almost immediately recognized the Polish volunteers as combatants within the framework of the Austrian army. This enterprise received a temporary setback when, on August 14, the Russian Grand Prince Nicholas, supreme commander of the Russian army, in a manifesto promised the Polish people complete unification under the Romanov scepter, and when, in the early fall, a large part of Galicia fell to the Russians. The fact, however, that eastern Galicia was treated by them as reconquered Russian territory weakened the trust of the pro-Russian section. In 1915 the Polish legions, by now considerably strengthened, participated effectively in the conquest of all of Russian Poland by the Central Powers. The high point of this trend of events seemed reached when, in November 1916, the German and Austrian governments solemnly proclaimed the establishment of a reconstituted Kingdom of Poland—in itself a fact of major importance for the Polish future. It thoroughly destroyed all chances for a separate peace between Russia and the Central Powers which would have been concluded, as before, by both sides sacrificing Polish claims to independence. The proclamation, on the other hand, made it difficult for the later policy of the Entente, and especially for America with its strong Polish population, to advocate anything less than full freedom for the Polish nation.

The immediate impact of the proclamation of Polish independence, however, was far less profitable than it sounded. Its main purpose had been the possibility of recruiting large numbers of Polish soldiers. Also it was strictly limited to Russian Poland (from whose territory, as it turned out later, the German high command even wanted to detach some border regions for annexation to Germany). The German demand that Polish soldiers should swear an oath of loyal "brotherhood" with the armies of the Central Powers led to a crisis within the Polish leadership. In its course Piłsudski resigned from his newly acquired position as a provisional minister of war within the Polish Council of State organized in January 1917 by the German-Austrian authorities, and was, in July, interned at Magdeburg. His break with the Germans strengthened enormously his moral position with the vast majority of Poles.

Meantime, the outbreak of the Russian revolution had opened up new vistas. In March 1917 the provisional Russian government proclaimed its readiness to acknowledge a free Poland, comprising all territories containing a majority of Poles. This act again forced the hand of the Central Powers who, in October, replaced the Council of State by a somewhat stronger Regency Council headed by Archbishop Kakowski of Warsaw and a cabinet of ministers. The new administrative apparatus soon functioned more effectively and, indeed, later facilitated the transition to real independence. This, of course, was bound up with the German collapse, and it was symbolic that on the day before the armistice Piłsudski was released and immediately took over the provisional headship of state of the republic which had been proclaimed on November 3. But the new state had still to undergo many difficulties and bloody struggles before it could be considered as firmly established within the framework of internationally acknowledged boundaries. Among the indubitably and overwhelmingly Polish territories that had to be gained against some armed resistance the first was the province (or, as it had been called, Grand Duchy) of Poznań, and this was achieved by Polish troops in the very last days of 1918. With that extension westward from the rump of former Russian Poland at least an essential step was taken toward the reconstruction of a true, united Poland. Yet there were other border problems of great difficulty, both east and west. As it turned out, the eastern problems were decided mainly by the sword, the western mainly at the conference table. And in personal terms this meant that the eastern decisions were influenced most decisively by Piłsudski, the western by Dmowski. Piłsudski was free Poland's first (provisional) head of state, but also, and for a much longer time, Poland's leading soldier. Dmowski had headed the Polish National Committee in Paris that had prepared the Western Allies for Polish restitution in work similar to that done by the Masaryk-Beneš-Štefánik triumvirate. There were still considerable differences between the opinions and goals of the two great Polish leaders. The man who had the tact, the charm, the recognized idealism, and the international prestige to bridge the gap was Paderewski. Having been made prime minister in Warsaw he joined Dmowski in Paris. There the Polish delegation fought for, and essentially obtained, a western border not unlike the one that Poland had had throughout much of her history as an independent state, specifically from the second Peace of Toruń in 1466 to the First Partition in 1772. Throughout those more than three hundred years, West Prussia (Royal Prussia) had been Polish and East Prussia, the Prussia of the Order (and later Ducal Prussia) an island surrounded by Polish land. The badly misnamed "Polish Corridor," which gave the new republic her exit to the sea, was thus by no means the politico-geographical and historical monstrosity it was presented as by a fiercely revisionist German propaganda throughout the interwar years. The most troublesome issue, in this connection, was Danzig, an old Hanseatic city that had long been a faithful daughter of the Polish crown. This, however, had been before the birth of modern nationalism. The city, dominating the mouth of the Vistula, Poland's great river, had been her main door for maritime entrance and exit, and could hardly be left outside her economic borders, even though ethnically it was overwhelmingly German. The solution—a free city, under League of

Nations protection, but within the Polish customs union—though not without historical precedent, was to create great difficulties. The German reaction was equally resentful in relation to Upper Silesia where a plebiscite resulted in slightly more than 700,000 votes for Germany and nearly half a million for Poland, an outcome that was reflected in a final decision of the League of Nations (1921) partitioning the province into a larger German and a somewhat smaller Polish territory. The latter, however, contained much of the great coal basin, including heavy industries built on it.

While Germany could, at this stage, only protest against the territorial losses sustained along Poland's western border, the eastern borders of Poland were the result of prolonged war conducted first between Poles and Ukrainians, later between Poles and Russians. The point of departure for those grim fights was the Polish demand, presented by Piłsudski, for the reestablishment of a large federal state under Polish leadership, but also including huge regions inhabited by non-Polish populations, among them Lithuania, Byelorussia and above all the Ukraine. The demand for such enormous eastward expansion was based on history and on the assumption (by Piłsudski and others) that the peoples concerned would be happy in a Polish-led state provided they could enjoy administrative autonomy. But the development of modern nationalism vitiated all such assumptions.

The great Russo-Polish War lasted only half a year (April to October 1920), but in this period the military situation underwent several striking changes. In the beginning the Poles seemed much superior and managed even to conquer Kiev, but were then driven back, with the Red Army invading central Poland as far as the Vistula. Yet in a great battle before the gates of Warsaw the Polish army, under Piłsudski, with some technical help from France, managed to defeat and partly destroy the invading Russian forces. The victorious Poles obtained, in the Peace of Riga (March 1921) a borderline far to the east of the ethnic border which the Western Allies, in the form of the so-called Curzon Line, had suggested. This large eastern expansion, though falling short of the 1772 border, included within the Polish borders many millions of Ukrainians, a fact which in the longer run weakened rather than strengthened the Polish state.

It could be foreseen that the new Poland, with its large areas claimed by Germans and Russians as by right theirs, would come under heavy pressure as soon as the two giants recovered from defeat and exhaustion. To some extent this was probably inevitable, and Poland's only strong hope to stand up to such dangers rested upon alliances, especially the alliance with victorious France, at the moment Europe's greatest military power. But Poland could probably also hope for close cooperation with the three states that eventually were to form the Little Entente and of which two, Czechoslovakia and Rumania, were her neighbors. Unfortunately, the relations between the new Poland and the new Czechoslovakia, two states so close to one another in ethnical terms and both equally threatened by a revisionist resumption of German eastward expansion, were badly marred at a very early stage of their independence. Among the ancient territories of the Bohemian crown which, after the Austro-Prussian wars of the eighteenth century, had remained in Hapsburg hands was the Duchy of Teschen (in Czech, Těšínsko; in Polish, Cieszyn). Its population, besides Czechs and Germans, was predominantly Polish. This relatively small territory had, however, great significance also because of its wealth of coal—the largest anywhere in the countries of the Crown of St. Wenceslas—and as a geographic link between Bohemia-Moravia and Slovakia. In the expansive mood that dominated both West Slav states during the early postwar period their new governments found it impossible to come to an agreement. As early as November 1918 Polish troops were sent to occupy much of the old duchy, and this territory given the right to vote in the first Polish elections in December. When diplomatic protests had no effect, the Czechs sent their own troops into the Teschen territory in January 1919, and since most of the Polish army was engaged in the east they had little difficulty in regaining the district in question. Both sides, in quickly using force to gain what they felt was by right theirs, surely committed a grave blunder, for it is clear enough that what each of them lost, the good will and possible alliance of the other, would in the long run have been of infinitely greater value for the maintenance of their independence than a few hundred square miles of land and a few tens of thousands of people. The outcome, more or less dictated to both sides in 1920 by the Entente powers still trying to liquidate the war, gave to Poland the greater eastern part of the duchy with the city of Teschen, to Czechoslovakia the railway line and the main part of the coal basin.

As, by this decision, some 80,000 Poles (more according to Polish statistics) remained under Czechoslovak rule, a Polish irredenta was created which, together with reactions on the other side of the border, badly damaged the relations between the countries during the following two decades.

THE NEW CZECHOSLOVAK STATE

We have still to sketch the events by which the Czechoslovak state was shaped. Recognition of the movement for independence from Hapsburg rule had come from all important Entente powers in the course of the summer of 1918, and in every case the Czechoslovak (or, as it was still frequently spelled, Czecho-Slovak) National Council in Paris was given recognition as "a de facto belligerent government, clothed with proper authority to direct the military and political affairs of the Czecho-Slovaks" (Declaration of the U.S. Department of State, September 2, 1918). The American recognition, that is, Wilson's support, was almost entirely due to Masaryk. To strengthen the moral support by Czech and Slovak Americans Masaryk also attended a meeting held at Pittsburgh on June 30, 1918, which endorsed the intention of creating a Czech-Slovak republic with a considerable measure of autonomy for Slovakia.

Meantime there had been a distinct growth of anti-Hapsburg feeling at home. As early as April 1917 all prominent Czech writers and poets, in a stirring manifesto, demanded a free and democratic Czech state within a thoroughly federalized empire. The young Emperor Charles, seeing his empire in a state of slow moral and political dissolution, tried to gain favor by the amnesty of Kramář, Alois Rašín, and other Czech leaders who had been sentenced to death for treason, but the carrot proved as ineffective as the stick—martial law was proclaimed in places where, as in the great industrial region of Ostrava, the workers had peacefully demonstrated and were shot at and several killed by German troops. The quiet revolution in the Czech countries could no longer be stopped but was rather enhanced by such brutality. On July 13, 1918, an interparty council called the National Committee headed by Karel Kramář for the National Democrats as president, and Antonín Švehla for the large Agrarian Party and Václav Klofáč for the National Socialists as vice-presidents, was founded and took up contact with the Paris Council. On May 1, a council of Slovak democrats and socialists had demanded "self-determination also for that branch of the Czechoslovak nation that lives in Hungary." The last attempts by the imperial government to save the empire by a manifesto proclaiming a federal realm (October 16) came far too late. On October 25 Kramář left Prague to meet Beneš in Geneva, but even before he could return, the other members of the Prague National Committee, with Vavro Šrobár as representative of the Slovaks, had on October 28 proclaimed "The Independent Czechoslovak State." This was followed, two days later, by a solemn declaration of independence signed by all Slovak leaders of all rank from all parties at a meeting in Turčiansky Svätý Martin, which said expressly: "The Slovak Nation is a part of the Czecho-Slovak Nation united in language and in the history of its culture. In all the cultural struggle which the Czech Nation has fought and which have made it known throughout the world, the Slovak Branch also participated."

Independence was achieved. But just as in the Polish case the question remained as to which territories should belong to the new country. For most Czech people, with their highly developed consciousness of history, any idea of splitting apart the lands of the Crown of St. Wenceslas was quite unbearable. The same, of course, was true for most Hungarians. But the Czechs and Slovaks were now on the side of the victorious powers, the Hungarians on that of the vanquished. The Czechs could claim that what had been wrong in the symbiosis of Czechs and Germans in the Bohemian territories had been the stubborn insistence of the German minority to occupy a dominating position, and they could promise—without history refuting them—that they would grant the Germans of Czechoslovakia cultural and economic freedom and, indeed, a measure of political influence that would make life in the republic somewhat better than bearable for them. Similar promises made in defense of the territorial integrity of the lands of the Crown of St. Stephen by the Magyars would fall on deaf ears; too long had reckless Magyarization been the generally accepted policy of all but a tiny minority of Magyar policy makers. Thus, while the Czechs could argue that not only historically, but also geographically, culturally, and economically, Bohemia and Moravia-Silesia formed a natural unit whose destruction would be a fatal blow to the country, and would render her quite incapable of military defense against her neighbors, it seemed understandable, if perhaps not strictly logical, that in the case of the Slovaks as in those of the Serbs, Rumanians, and Ruthenians, ethnic rather than historical criteria were to determine the new border lines. Thus, while the two western countries maintained their ancient borders, with merely minute changes in two or three cases, the Slovak-Hungarian border, apart from some 90 miles along the Danube, cut through the northern rim of the great central-Danubian plain, enclosing some 700,000 Magyars on Slovak territory, but leaving also some 140,000 Slovaks, not all in immediate proximity to the northern border, in Hungary. The Ruthenians of Hungary, separated from the bulk of their Ukrainian relatives by the Carpathian mountains and a large stretch of Polish territory, also requested incorporation in Czechoslovakia with a degree of autonomy, first through its representatives in the United States, then through "national councils" at home. This extremely poor and backward region became, in the following years, a sort of Czech mandate with more burdens than advantages for the republic, though it was valued by Prague as a territorial bridge connecting Czechoslovakia with her ally Rumania. In fact the Ruthenians, though a good deal was done for them and all attempts at their denationalization ceased, added to the already large proportion of never quite satisfied ethnic minorities in the country—altogether about a third of the population of 13,600,000, among whom slightly more than three million were Germans, now usually called Sudeten Germans.

The strong proportion of ethnic minorities—in each case about one third of the total population—was indeed, together with their exposed geographic position, the greatest weakness of both reborn nations of East Central Europe. The question how they would deal with this problem would have a considerable influence upon their future development.

TWO DECADES OF FREEDOM

The period from the end of World War I to the prelude to World War II, which occurred, with the events of October 1938, exactly 20 years later—this short, precious period of national freedom—showed a different face in the two West Slav states. True, they had much in common. Both had emerged from a long time in which they had been deprived of their free political existence; both had shown their tenacious will to maintain and develop their nationhood, and had finally prevailed; both were burdened with large national minorities which were the more dangerous as they could look across the border to the larger populations to whom ethnically they belonged; both had to try to obtain a minimum of security by joining and to some extent creating systems of alliances which, so it was hoped, would keep their potential enemies in check.

But there were also great differences. Czechoslovakia, in terms of territory and population, was a small, or at best a medium-sized, state that could not expect to play anything like a leading role in European politics, though her statesmen enjoyed, for a while, a remarkable respect in the international forum of the League of Nations. Poland, with almost three times the area and more than twice the population—indeed, the fourth most populous country on the European continent west of the Soviet Union (after Germany, France, and Italy)—could perhaps think of herself as being on the way toward becoming a great power, a chance that seemed possible at a moment when her two traditional enemy neighbors were both weakened to an unusual degree. In other ways, however, it was Czechoslovakia that appeared stronger and sounder. For one thing, of course, she had not suffered from the war as badly as had Poland, as there had been no fighting on her soil. Above all, Czechoslovakia was economically more highly developed and had, on the average, a higher standard of living, though in both countries the western regions were richer than those of the east. True, Poland had great industrial centers in Upper Silesia, in Łódź, and near Warsaw, but in Bohemia and Moravia industrialization had made far greater progress during the later nineteenth and early twentieth centuries than in Poland, and the proportion of people living in cities or employed in industrial enterprises—as compared to the farming sector of the population—was far greater. Bohemia and Moravia had been the main industrial arsenal for the whole of the vast Hapsburg Empire. This was, however, not wholly a source of strength, since the erection of new customs barriers across the large territory of the former Hapsburg monarchy would deprive Czechoslovakia's industry of some important markets. In fact this led soon to attempts to gain new markets in other regions, in Europe and also overseas. But this increased dependence on exports, though an expression of the high standard of the country's technological development, made her also, as it turned out, more susceptible to losses resulting from economic ills in other countries.

Even so, there is no question that, economically, Czechoslovakia was far better off than Poland. And while both countries were, in the first phase after the war, hit by the great wave of inflation that swept almost all of Europe, Czechoslovakia, under the leadership of her careful and energetic minister of finance, Alois Rašín, managed to separate the Czechoslovak koruna from that of the other succession states as early as February 1919, and by restricting the paper circulation generally maintained its value—not, indeed, without initial sacrifice—throughout the life of the republic, thereby making an important contribution to general stability. In Poland, on the other hand, the inflation went on for years and was only stopped—by the energetic nonpartisan Prime Minister Grabski—in 1923, but only temporarily. It was not until 1927 that, with the help of an American loan, the złoty was more permanently stabilized.

To some extent those financial troubles reflected the extraordinary difficulties which the country had to overcome in the task of reconstruction. Not only had industries and houses to be rebuilt but, symbolizing the basic task, three entirely different railroad systems had to be connected and unified. The fact that they had different gauges was less important than that they had served different, largely strategic purposes. It was characteristic, for instance, that from the great industrial region of Upper Silesia with its huge coal deposits, which offered one of the most important exportable products of the country, there was no direct connection with their main outlet at the Baltic sea region. The building of a new railroad connecting north and south thus became one of the most valuable additions to the Polish transport system. It notably facilitated the export of coal to Scandinavia, an important customer who had switched to Polish coal especially during the great strike of the British coal miners (May to November 1926). The northern terminus of this great trunk line was not Danzig—the city that had been separated from Germany to give the Polish foreign trade an adequate sea port. Instead Poland had, when Danzig was not actually incorporated into Poland, soon begun to build her own port city at Gdynia, in 1919 merely a small fishing village some 15 miles northwest of Danzig. The creation of this port (and of a fairly strong Polish merchant navy) was an extraordinary achievement. In a relatively short time Gdynia had not only overtaken Danzig in terms of capacity and actual volume of shipping, but had become one of Europe's leading port cities and an attractive metropolis to boot. While its development was, of course, much resented in Danzig and in parts of Germany, the Nazis were eventually to pay a sort of odd compliment to this constructive creation when, all through World War II, they made more use of Gdynia (renamed "Gotenhafen") than of any other Baltic port.

There were other constructive works which belong to this phase: a rapid build-up of an adequate system of education from elementary schools up to universities where it was badly needed, that is, in the territories which had belonged to Russia and Germany; rather progressive labor legislation; and laws regarding land reform which, however, proceeded rather slowly and permitted much larger estates to survive in the east, where the land-hungry peasants were mostly Ukrainians and the landowners not infrequently Poles.

The problem of the minorities was indeed one which was to plague Poland throughout those two decades. The most important of them were, in the order of their size, Ukrainians, Jews, and Germans. A special problem existed in relation to Lithuanians, whose total number in Poland was not very great but the majority of whom had completely ceased to consider themselves as co-heirs of the old Polish-Lithuanian federation. They had now obtained their own national state, but the Poles, in 1920, had seized Vilna (Polish Wilno), a city of many nations, mostly Jews, Poles, and Lithuanians, of which none had an absolute majority. Culturally it meant much to the Poles, but the Lithuanians, claiming the town as their ancient capital, never forgave the Poles, and until 1938 there was a "cold war" between both nations that was expressed in a closed border and a complete lack of any relations, diplomatic or economic.

Of the three great minorities, the Jewish one was the only one which could not be or become the instrument of an irredentist policy. Indeed, there were many Jews who would have been extremely unwilling to be counted as a national minority and who felt themselves to be patriotic Poles. They were, however, a minority, as against a larger group, whose Yiddish language and Jewish cultural tradition was strictly defined and not open to any degree of assimilation. The process by which Poland, under the Jagellons one of the most tolerant of nations, had become infected by a considerable measure of anti-Semitism cannot be discussed here. Of the leaders of the nation, the historically most important, Marshal Piłsudski, was himself free from such prejudice, but as democracy slowly vanished in the country the anti-Semitic poison began to spread more visibly. (The "Jewish question," of course, was most thoroughly "solved" not by the Poles but by the German occupation after 1939.) The Ukrainian minority—it was indeed a majority in large parts of Poland's east and southeast—had been annexed by the Peace of Riga without having had the slightest chance of expressing its own wishes. At the same time very little was done to give this large mass of people a feeling that they had any degree of cultural and economic freedom and self-determination, let alone of political influence, such as the Ukrainians had originally been promised (in Piłsudski's case probably in good faith) when the Poles tried to gain, in 1920, the whole of Ukraine. Some Polish government circles rather hoped to polonize at least part of the Ukrainians, in challenge to the minority treaties which the Polish government had signed, albeit grudgingly, during the Paris peace negotiations. The deep dissatisfaction with this policy led to the development of a strongly nationalist and autonomist movement in eastern Galicia, and after 1930 this took the form of terrorist acts, which were answered with very severe measures of suppression by the government.

If these conflicts were bound to create difficulties also in Polish-Russian relations, no great suppression was needed to create difficulties with the German neighbor. The German minority, only some 800,000 strong, could hardly make claims for autonomy in the same way as the seven times stronger Ukrainian people in Poland. But the Germans had the special grudge of a majority turned into a minority, and the deep conviction that the loss, if not of Poznania, then at least of West Prussia and upper Silesia was absurd, immoral, and clearly ephemeral. On this the Germans in Poland were at one with most people in Germany. Thus it might well be said that even if the treatment of the German minority had been exemplary—which was by no means the case—it would not have reconciled those people with the new borders and especially with the so-called Polish Corridor.

The Polish attitude toward the minority treaties had been sharply critical from the beginning, and in 1934 they were unilaterally repudiated by Warsaw. Prague's policy, in this regard, was very different. True, occasional utterances in the beginning that Czechoslovakia would try to be another Switzerland were not really put into effect. On the other hand, it is probably fair to say that in no other Central or East European country were the rights and just claims of national minorities respected as much as in Czechoslovakia. The theory behind the minorities policy of the Czechoslovak government was that the new republic was indeed the national state of Czechs and Slovaks, but that national minorities, if not actually equal in influence to the Slavic "state nations," among whom, in Ruthenia, the Ukrainian majority was also counted, would still have all the rights, freedoms, and amenities that would make their life within the republic much better than tolerable, and would enable them to develop a feeling of loyalty to this state.

It is not quite easy to say exactly to what extent these intentions were in fact implemented. It is, of course, possible to quote a number of facts that indicated a remarkable degree of freedom, especially for the greatest and most important minority, the 3.2 millions of Germans. Among these was the existence of a strong and fully state-supported system of education from the smallest village school to the German University in Prague and two technological institutes, in Prague and in Brno, also of university standard. There were state subsidies for other cultural institutions, such as theaters. There was a large and unfettered German press in Prague as well as in the provinces. Germans were represented in Parliament, essentially in proportion to their total strength and organized in a number of parties from the Socialist left (the Communists had no national divisions) to the farthest, most nationalist right. From 1926 two or three of the so-called "activist" German parties had their representatives in the cabinet, often in positions of considerable influence, including the Ministry of Justice. Compared to the fate of almost all other European national minorities this seemed sheer paradise.

Yet in fairness it should be said that there were some less admirable features. In particular many of the ruling Czech bureaucrats enjoyed and occasionally abused in their administrative practice their newly gained power, and on such issues especially as the handling of language decrees a policy of pinpricks often resulted in antagonisms which a wise policy might well have avoided. Yet when all is said the fact remains that especially in the years from 1926 to 1931, before the depression became fully effective in Czechoslovakia, a definite majority of Germans had begun to put up with their place in the republic and to acknowledge the fact that a partition of Bohemia was neither feasible nor desirable. They would probably have become even less inclined to a policy of opposition on principle if the economic situation and with it the political atmosphere in all of Europe had remained what it had appeared to be in the second half of the twenties—fairly prosperous and healthy. On the other hand, from the time of the Nazi revolution in Germany, Sudeten German disaffection was carefully nurtured from Berlin, and it was, of course, aggravated by the fact that the Sudeten German industries, working to a high degree for export, were hurt, especially by the impact of the world depression of the early thirties.

Compared with the Sudeten German questions those of the other minorities—the Magyars in Slovakia and Ruthenia and the small Polish minority in Silesia—seemed very secondary. Yet the republic had another problem that was of considerable difficulty, especially once she came under the crossfire of ill intentioned neighbors—the development of the relationship between Czechs and Slovaks.

We have shown earlier that the Slovak contribution to the spiritual awakening of the early and mid-nineteenth century was considerable and on a very high level. On the other hand, the survival of Slovak nationhood and civilization had, in the last decades of the Hapsburg Empire and of the Hungarian policy of extreme Magyarization, become increasingly doubtful. The total destruction of the Slovak educational system with its respectable traditions, both Catholic and Protestant, had endangered the very life of the Slovak intelligentsia, which had become a good deal smaller and less effective in 1918 than it had been 50 years earlier. Twenty years after 1918 the Slovak intelligentsia had multiplied in size and considerably improved in depth and competence. The two decades of the existence of the Czechoslovak Republic had rescued the Slovaks and their civilization from the acute danger of destruction. And it is clear enough that this important rescue could never have been performed without the strong and indeed eager support of the Czechs.

Yet this rescue operation, in itself, was bound to some extent to result in misunderstandings between the two sides and, indeed, in resentment on the side of the Slovaks. The Czechs who were sent to Slovakia to help run the administration, build up a new and comprehensive system of education, and to lift the artificially depressed standards of "Upper Hungary" to the far higher ones of Bohemia and Moravia, were mostly well meaning and competent. The very fact that in 1939 a separate Slovak state could somehow exist where it would have been an impossibility twenty years earlier shows that the Slovaks had not only been able students but had also had able teachers. Many of these returned to the West when it appeared that their work had been done, others married Slovak wives and became half Slovak themselves. But even a minority among them who were sufficiently convinced of their superiority to show arrogance and lack of understanding for Slovak pride would spoil the atmosphere. Another disturbing element arose from the different religious attitudes of Czechs and Slovaks. While in both regions there were strong Catholic majorities, they were different. The Czechs, somewhat like the French, could be Catholic and yet distinctly anticlerical. For the Slovak Catholics, much as for those of Poland, their religion encompassed much more of their whole existence. The great Hussite tradition could be and was a source of pride for Catholic Czechs, but much less so for Catholic Slovaks. The Catholic church had, on the whole, been a supporter of the Magyar regime in the prewar period. This, perhaps, was understandable. But there were also a few influential Catholics of Slovak origin who before the war had become complete renegades toward Magyarism and were now quite willing to serve this cause, or their own glorification, by trying to pull the Slovak people back from the Czechoslovak to a Magyar orientation. Small though their number was, it sufficed to do considerable harm. In the beginning, the most active among these people was Father F. Jehlička, who had, after a short career as a Slovak patriot, refrained from further such actions upon the orders of the Archbishop of Esztergom and now emerged again, supposedly to watch over the real freedoms of the Slovak people. His voice was later heard over a Vienna radio station paid by Budapest, and in 1933 he made his Magyar orientation more obvious by accompanying the prime minister of Hungary on a propaganda trip to England. While his direct influence appears to have been limited, he was able to do great mischief through his effect on some other influential men. Among them was Dr. Adalbert Tuka, before the war a professor of law at the Magyar University of Pozsony (Bratislava). He had, in 1921, declared himself as a Magyar but was nevertheless permitted to become editor of *Slovak*, the official paper of Andrew Hlinka's autonomist party. His role in the following years was wholly negative and destructive, and in 1929 he was put on trial for treason and espionage for a foreign power and was sentenced to 15 years of prison. He emerged a happy victor in the Hitler-created "independent" Slovakia when in his role as prime minister and foreign minister he identified himself and his nation completely with the ideas and ideals of the Nazi party.

The real tragedy was that both of these, Jehlička as well as Tuka, had at one time real influence upon the man who was, without any doubt, at heart a true Slovak patriot, Father Andrew Hlinka. It was Jehlička who persuaded this somewhat hot-blooded and impulsive priest to protest in person, in September 1919, to the Peace Conference in Paris against the fact that the statements of the Pittsburgh Convention, presented now as a binding international treaty, had not been kept by the Czechs. This procedure, of course, made the relationship between Hlinka and the Prague government—but also between Hlinka and the nonautonomist groups among Slovak leaders and politicians—difficult.

Yet Hlinka, and with him the more reasonable men in his "Slovak People's Party" had some basis for justified complaint. The cutting off of the old markets of Slovakia—Central Hungary with Budapest—caused economic difficulties to which the Prague government did not always pay sufficient attention. To blame the Czechs for using the term "Czechoslovak nation," as was and is often done by Anti-Czech Slovaks, is hardly fair when this term was used so emphatically in the great Declaration of Independence adopted by all Slovak leaders at Turčiansky Svätý Martin in October 1918, and when so many people among the Czechs and at least a minority among the Slovaks thought of themselves quite sincerely as belonging to the Czechoslovak nation. Something else, however, was the steady usage of the term "Czechoslovak language" which indeed was nothing but a fiction. And the Czech leaders, including even Masaryk, were hardly right in minimizing, as they did repeatedly, their moral obligations arising out of the agreement of Pittsburgh which demanded a considerable measure of true autonomy for Slovakia. It was then most irking, even for many "Czechoslovak-thinking" Slovaks, that during the first years of the Republic there was no administrative unit for the whole of Slovakia, as the Republic had been divided into smaller districts called *župy*. This system, largely in answer to Slovak demands, was reformed in 1927 so as to create four large separate provinces—Bohemia, Moravia-Silesia, Slovakia, and Ruthenia—each with its own provincial diet which was a counterweight of some, though not always enough, effectiveness against overly centralizing tendencies in Prague. There had, of course, never been a government without Slovak representation in important offices, but in January 1927 the Slovak People's Party, too, was allowed by Father Hlinka to send two of its members into the cabinet. As the People's Party was the largest single party in Slovakia (though it always remained a minority, polling, with ups and downs, usually about one third of the total) its entry into the government promised a considerable degree of stabilization. It was unfortunate that at the time of the Tuka trial Father Hlinka felt that he should publicly back Tuka. Thereupon, in the immediately following elections in late October 1929, the People's Party lost heavily. From then until the end of the first republic it remained in opposition, steadfastly claiming, against all evidence, that it, and it alone, was the true voice of the Slovak people—against all evidence, since the contribution of patriotic Slovaks to the development of their narrower homeland and the whole republic continued to be remarkable. It should have been culminated when in 1935 Dr. Milan Hodža, the strongest personality among Slovak statesmen, an old fighter for Slovak freedom in Magyar days, and one of the initiators of the idea of the international cooperation of European peasant parties, became prime minister. That his stewardship ended in tragedy—the tragedy of Munich—was certainly not his fault.

Even before the beginning of his premiership, and the almost simultaneous resignation of President Masaryk and the succession of Dr. Beneš, there had been occasional crises brought about by political dissension, twice overcome by the president installing a temporary government consisting entirely of permanent civil servants. But on the whole the system of government by coalition, with the prime minister taken from the largest single party—first the Social Democrats, later the Agrarians—functioned remarkably well, even under the special difficulties presented by the impact of the international depression upon Czechoslovakia's economy. There was never any real danger, in those years, for the continued vigorous existence of a working democratic system. The fairly strong Communist Party (in the elections of 1925 it became temporarily the second strongest), concentrated its attacks mainly on issues of social policy, and the vocal but weak Czech Fascists, split in two groups, were hardly taken seriously. On the whole, the stability of the Czechoslovak democratic system was all the more remarkable as not a single one of her direct neighbors or of the other nations of Central, East Central, and Southeastern Europe managed, in the interwar years, to avoid the slippery road toward some form of dictatorship.

This, unfortunately, was also true for Poland. Even more than Czechoslovakia's constitution, which had adopted some elements from the United States, Poland's constitution of 1920 was largely a copy of that of France's Third Republic. Like France, therefore—but without the relative sturdiness derived from long tradition and a highly competent civil service—Poland suffered from incessant cabinet crises and increasing difficulties of the parliamentary parties to work together. It was dissatisfaction of a large part of the people, including the workers and their organizations, that in May 1926 supported Marshal Piłsudski's open rebellion against the government of President Wojciechowski and the prime minister, Wincenty Witos, whose strong agrarian policy had made him the object of much admiration and much hostility. But if Piłsudski, having achieved all the substance of decisive power, seemed to want to fight rightist reaction with the help of his old friends, the Socialists, it soon became clear that he fought against all parties and against the very idea of a parliamentary democracy, for which the gruff old soldier had nothing but contempt. In 1930 he arrested all the more highly respected party leaders, men who had suffered for Poland's freedom, among them the Social Democrat Lieberman and the Agrarian Witos. The latter, eventually, found asylum in Czechoslovakia, where his friend Hodža was prime minister.

If for a while, with Piłsudski's friend Moscicki in the presidency, at least the façade of the parliamentary system was maintained, this was no longer true when in March 1935 a new constitution was imposed. It gave the president, as head of the executive department, unlimited power, eliminated the parties as bodies able to nominate candidates for the *Sejm* (who were now nominated through a sort of corporate system partly borrowed from Italy), and made the Senate a largely appointive body, thus turning Parliament into a mere rubberstamp institution. When, soon after, Piłsudski died, power remained in the hands of a clique of military men (together with some bureaucrats), usually simply called "the Colonels." What separated it from true Fascism was the absence of a large and effective fascist party. Colonel Adam Koc's "Camp of National Unity," and its more radical successor, the "Union of Young Poland," were intended to provide some such broad basis but did not really succeed, in spite of the adoption of that extreme nationalism and even anti-Semitism that was so effective at this time in neighboring Germany. While it was, undoubtedly, an authoritarian regime in which the last decisions were made by small and uncontrolled groups of officers and civil servants, opposition could never be completely stamped out and it expressed itself in widespread strikes of peasants and industrial workers, some of which were suppressed by military force. What made all domestic issues appear secondary was the increasingly critical situation in Europe, above all the expansionist moves of the great totalitarian systems in Italy and Germany. The two West Slav powers tried to handle them in radically different ways, yet both were fated to become, in short sequence, their victims.

EIGHT

The Tragedy: Bankrupt Foreign Policy and Nazi Occupation

Historians have in the past, and indeed generations ago, described the history of the smaller Slavic nations as beset by tragedy. The developments culminating in World War II and its aftermath seem to confirm this impression. There were a good many nations which became victims of Hitler's conquest, but most of them, Denmark and Norway, France and the Low Countries, even Greece, were at least not subject to a treatment which questioned, indeed negated, their very existence as nations. This, however, was what happened to Czechoslovakia and Poland. It appeared for a while as if both had achieved freedom from prolonged subjection in 1918 only to be deprived of it in a far more horrible and final way in the year from October 1938 to October 1939.

That their independence was based on precarious foundations and needed to be especially buttressed by relations to friendly nations was clear to the Polish and Czechoslovak statesmen who shouldered the responsibility for their countries' foreign relations. For both it seemed almost a matter of course that they had to base their policy on intimate friendship and cooperation with France. This was not only a result of military geography but was just as firmly based on old traditions of political friendship. A close cooperation between France and the eastern European states that had sided with the Entente during the great war was one of the ways in which the leading French statesmen, above all Clemenceau, tried to establish France's dominant position on the continent. But such a system was also designed to give all of Europe a security and steadiness which had everything to gain from firm stabilization of the map, specifically of the border lines, which had emerged after the war. It was clear from the beginning that this settlement would not be recognized as permanent by the defeated nations—Germany, Hungary, and Bulgaria (Turkey's case was in many ways different). In the case of Poland three of her five neighbors—Germany, Russia, and Lithuania, the first two potentially, if not actually, Europe's strongest powers—were deeply dissatisfied and hoped for a more or less radical border revision. In Czechoslovakia's case the most obvious enemy was Hungary, whose revisionist policy became already clear through the early attempt of her Communist dictator Béla Kun to reconquer Slovakia. It was Hungary's constant propaganda against all her neighbors, but especially Czechoslovakia, Rumania, and Yugoslavia, that induced those three to conclude with each other an alliance, which was strengthened by the fact that all three were allies of France and that a strict and general maintenance of the *status quo* would safeguard all of them not only against Hungary but also against other neighbors, such as Russia in the case of Rumania, and Bulgaria in the case of both Rumania and Yugoslavia. For Czechoslovakia, of course, the most formidable potential enemy was Germany. But in the early years, and indeed up to 1933, Germany was not really an acute danger. German revisionism, strong as it was even after 1919, was clearly based on the conception of German borders as they had existed from 1871 to 1918. Even the "grossdeutsche" conception of a Germany which would include Austria, while quite alive, especially among Socialists, was nowhere nearly as strong an emotional issue as was, say, the "Polish Corridor." While there was pan-Germanism alive among right-wing Sudeten Germans, there was hardly any German irredentism regarding the Sudeten German territories in the Reich itself where this border, unchanged (except for a minute correction) for many centuries, was regarded as normal. Consequently, relations between Prague and Berlin, while not exactly cordial, were at least quite correct and most of the time unencumbered by any particularly difficult issues. It is perhaps ironical that one reproach to which the Czechoslovak government and its permanent Foreign Minister Dr. Beneš were occasionally subjected by German political opinion was his willingness, in issues concerning German-Polish relations, to take the side of Poland. Beneš had, indeed, patiently made strenuous efforts to overcome the deep alienation between the two West Slav powers that had resulted from the Těšín issue, and in 1925, at a time when the Warsaw foreign office was in the capable hands of Count Alexander Skrzyński, he seemed to succeed. At a visit in Warsaw three agreements were signed which were intended to smooth over all disputes and to enable the two powers to cooperate closely on such decisive issues as East Central Europe's position in relation to the Locarno treaties. Beneš had earlier tried to strengthen the idea of collective security in Europe by sponsoring and drafting, at the League of Nations, the Geneva Protocol, which would have provided compulsory arbitration of all international disputes and a clear designation of nations refusing to submit to arbitration as aggressors liable to be punished. Britain's new Conservative government had caused this great scheme to fall, and the Locarno treaties which were supposed to take its place seemed to limit firm guaranties to Germany's western borders. It was the common action of Prague and Warsaw which salvaged the situation at least partly by the conclusion of arbitration treaties between Germany and her two eastern neighbors, and by the simultaneous conclusion of Franco-Polish and Franco-Czechoslovak treaties of mutual assistance in case of a German attack. Thus, in spite of the originally very critical feelings about Locarno in both West Slav states, it could be said that their international position had been strengthened by what appeared to be a notable consolidation of the ties between Warsaw and Prague (or Warsaw and the Little Entente) and between Paris and all the smaller Eastern powers interested in the maintenance of the *status quo*.

This happy state did not last very long. The period of Polish-Czechoslovak friendship and cooperation was especially short, since it was dropped as soon as Piłsudski, always a Czechophobe, took over the reigns of government by the coup of 1926.

Piłsudski did not believe in collective security as a policy. He thought little of the League of Nations and disliked Germany's entry into this body, especially when it appeared that Germany, but not Poland, would receive a permanent seat in the League's Council. Eventually Poland had to be satisfied with a "semi-permanent" seat, that is, the right to be reelected to the Council.

A radical change in the picture of Europe's international relations was, however, brought about by Hitler's accession to power in Germany. In contrast to his predecessors the former Austrian had an active dislike for Czechoslovakia, and soon the Nazis began to make full use of the radical nationalists within the German minority as a fifth column. From now on Prague had reason to regard Germany not merely as a potential but as a real danger, especially since from now on the Nazis vigorously increased their subversive work in Austria.

On the other hand Germany's policy toward Poland—against whom the Nazis, prior to coming to power, had conducted an especially vicious propaganda campaign—seemed to undergo a complete change of tone: Hitler, the simple soldier of the World War, solemnly offered the hand of friendship to Marshal Piłsudski, another old soldier. He did what would have been impossible to anybody else: the new Germany, so he declared, acknowledged that a nation of 35 millions could not exist without a free exit to the sea. It is difficult to blame Piłsudski for the fact that, after informing France, he accepted the ten-year nonaggression pact offered by the Nazis. At the moment it seemed to lead to an effective reduction of the international tension under which Poland had suffered. Ten years of guaranteed peace, so it was felt, was worth taking the risk that was implied in the cooling off of the old French friendship. Indeed, both Piłsudski and his new foreign minister, Colonel Józef Beck, had a very low opinion of contemporary France's fiber which, unfortunately, was in part justified, and an even lower opinion of Czechoslovakia, which was not nearly as justified. The two West Slav powers now went radically different ways: Poland, with Colonel Beck completely in charge after Piłsudski's death, took the way of steady *rapprochement* toward the camp of revisionist powers headed by Germany and Italy and including Hungary; Czechoslovakia, essentially guided as before by Dr. Beneš, even after he had followed Masaryk as president, took the way of trying to widen and thereby solidify the camp of those powers which might have the strength, through full cooperation, to contain the dangers of a wildly revisionist imperialism. It is easy to point out that the one policy collapsed just as thoroughly as the other. But this does not imply an acknowledgment of the claim that both policies were equally wrong. For Beck's policy, based, as it was, on the naïve expectation that the Nazi regime had really given up the older revisionist goals as far as Poland was concerned—this attempt at riding the tiger—was, as all such attempts are, suicidal. Beneš's policy, on the contrary, was the only one that might have saved his country if the Western powers, especially England and

France, had seen the signs as clearly as Beneš. There was, at least, one important French statesman whose views were almost identical with Beneš': Louis Barthou, who became foreign minister early in 1934 and who immediately tried to achieve an understanding with Russia. The main immediate result was Russia's joining the League of Nations, and on May 2, 1935, France and the Soviet Union concluded a pact of mutual assistance, followed, two weeks later, by a similar treaty between Czechoslovakia and Russia, which obliged Moscow to come to Czechoslovakia's aid as long as France, too, did so. While this step was not followed by corresponding acts of the other two members of the Little Entente, it was nevertheless approved by them and especially by Rumania.

But the hope thereby to contain the two fascist powers effectively was, before too long, dashed. When Hitler, in March 1936, denounced the Locarno Pact and reoccupied the Rhineland, France, under British pressure, far from drawing the necessary conclusions, limited herself to a paper protest. From now on the cause of collective security was lost. The League of Nations, after Italy had defied the policy of sanctions in the Ethiopian crisis, forfeited all strength and prestige. The Western powers, in their actions regarding the Spanish Civil War, showed only their growing willingness to be "realistic" and retreat step by step before the Axis offensive. The worst blow for Czechoslovakia was, in March 1938, the annexation of Austria to Germany, an act which put her into an almost hopeless strategic position. Immediately after this Hitlerian triumph began the direct assault of Germany against Czechoslovakia, first in the form of using the huge fifth column which the Nazis had been able to organize in the border regions of Czechoslovakia—the "Sudeten German Party" led by Konrad Henlein.

The German propaganda offensive against Czechoslovakia had started long before, but had been turned on and off according to what Hitler considered opportune. It had been completely quiet during the early months of 1938 but was resumed full blast after Austria's annexation, in the expectation thereby not only to intimidate Prague but also to prepare her Western allies for the need of far-reaching concessions. In view of the basic attitudes of Britain's Prime Minister Neville Chamberlain this campaign was largely successful. A setback for Germany resulted when an increase in the threatening German propaganda and rumors about German troop movements in Saxony near the Czech border led, on May 20, to a partial mobilization of Czechoslovak army units which made some international impression by the smooth way in which all units, including members of the minorities, followed the call-up. But the presentation, by parts of the world press, of the event as a defeat for Hitler was a mistake. So, however, was the later claim that only now Hitler definitely decided to destroy his small neighbor—this decision had been taken by him at the latest toward the end of 1936. In any case the game—with the Sudeten Germans steadily increasing their demands while Prague, under increasing pressure from London and Paris, tried to come to some agreement with them—continued until Chamberlain forced upon the Czech government the acceptance of a commission, headed by Lord Runciman, which was supposed to act as a mediator, but which in fact gave a distinct boost to Henlein and his party. In September Chamberlain, in order to maintain peace with Germany at absolutely any price the Czechs could be forced to pay, continued to play Hitler's game for him. After two visits to Germany the final arrangement was made at a conference convened, upon Mussolini's suggestion, at Munich in September 1938 at which Chamberlain and Daladier of France signed Czechoslovakia's, and with it to a large extent their own, capitulation to the Nazi chieftain. For the Czechoslovak government there was, short of national suicide, little choice but resignation. The Russian alliance was tied to the French one, and even if Moscow had been ready to support, on her own, her small ally militarily, she had no common border with Czechoslovakia.

As a result of Munich, Germany gained large areas to the north, west, and south of Bohemia and Moravia, containing, with the bulk of the Sudeten Germans, also about 820,000 Czechs, a quarter of the population of the ceded lands. The territory also included all the strong fortifications built during the earlier years upon the suggestion and with the participation of the French army, and all the matériel contained therein. Hungary, who had originally hoped to gain all or most of Slovakia, had to be satisfied with a long stretch in the south of Slovakia containing half a million Magyars but also almost 300,000 Slovaks. While Hungary received this directly through the benevolence of Hitler, Poland's government, completely guided by Józef

Beck, decided to imitate Hitler as closely as possible. After having earlier refused a Czechoslovak offer of negotiations he presented, in September 1938, a harshly worded ultimatum which the Czechs, in their total helplessness, had to accept. It gave to Poland a land with less than 80,000 Poles and more than 100,000 Czechs. Churchill was not the only one who characterized this act as hyenalike, and a great Polish historian called it a "most regrettable step," which "on Poland was notably avenged." The first indications that the bill would soon be presented came, indeed, almost immediately. But meantime Czechoslovakia's ordeal was far from over.

Hitler was not satisfied with having destroyed Czechoslovakia's true independence and her ability to withstand his plans for further eastward expansion; he decided to annex the western part of the country and to transform its eastern part, Slovakia, into a German puppet state. The means were the same as before. The Czechoslovak government, after the Munich debacle and Dr. Beneš's resignation, had been totally transformed with the goal of causing Berlin as little irritation as humanly possible. A man of the extreme right of the Agrarian Party, Rudolf Beran, became prime minister, while Emil Hácha, an old conservative jurist, was made president. The democratic structure of Czech political life was done away with, and in Slovakia the People's Party of Hlinka, led after his death by Msgr. Tiso, gained the chance to form the government of a fully autonomous Slovak province or state. But the relative stability which, astonishingly enough, appeared to be possible throughout much of the winter in the cruelly mutilated country, was not what Hitler wanted. Early in 1939 Nazi agitators got busy trying to goad feelings in Slovakia toward separation. Accordingly, as early as February the notorious Dr. Tuka declared at a reception by Hitler that he entrusted the fate of his people to him. Soon after this the German chargé d'affaires in Prague was ordered to warn the Czech government about impending Slovak separatist moves and to encourage them to take energetic steps against them. President Hácha, perhaps naïvely, followed the advice and deposed Tiso, replacing him by Karol Sidor, long one of the leading protagonists of Slovak autonomism but not a separatist. Now Hitler took over. He presented the heads of Tiso's party with the alternative of either declaring immediately for independence from the Czechs or else being annexed by Hungary. This revolting intrigue marked the birth of that supposedly sovereign Slovak republic which immediately requested, and just as quickly obtained, the solemn assurance of being a state under Hitler's permanent military protection, in other words a German protectorate. The further development of this state—the creation of a one-party regime, of a powerful paramilitary organization, of concentration camps, and even, under German command and against some resistance on the part of leading Slovaks, of a policy of liquidating the Jewish population—proved that Dr. Tuka, soon the most powerful man in Slovakia, was right when he solemnly promised that Slovakia would soon be "a modern National Socialist state."

The official term "protectorate," however, was reserved by the Nazis for Bohemia and Moravia, the two western countries which were occupied without any possible chance for resistance on March 14 and 15. The two provinces supposedly would have autonomy within the framework of the Greater German Empire. In fact this was, from the beginning, a military occupation in which the Gestapo was constantly busy trying to stamp out the resistance which, before long, took the form of sabotaging the German war effort. The acquisition of Czechoslovakia's heavy industry, and particularly of such great arms manufacturers as the Škoda Works in Pilsen and the Zbrojovka in Brno, were indeed one of the huge gains for Hitler which the Western powers had decided to neglect when they delivered Czechoslovakia into the hands of the Nazis.

The occupation of Prague and of rump-Czechoslovakia, however, had finally opened the eyes even of most of the eager appeasers in the West. As if to make sure that they would not forget this frightening lesson, Hitler immediately proceeded to address himself to the next victim on his list—Poland.

Hitler's first step toward "solving" the Polish problem had been taken immediately after Munich, on October 24, when, in as yet a polite form, the following suggestions were made to the Polish government: Poland agrees to Germany annexing Danzig; she permits the building of a "corridor through the corridor," that is, a strip of land containing a double-track railroad and an *Autobahn* with extraterritorial rights, connecting Danzig and East Prussia with German Pomerania; she joins the Anti-Comintern Pact against the Soviet Union. In return Germany is ready to extend the Treaty of 1934 to last 20 years and guarantee Poland's borders. For the next few weeks this proposal was repeatedly presented to Beck. His answer was that he was ready to negotiate on the issues in question, that he was willing, in particular, to replace the League's guaranty for Danzig by a direct German-Polish agreement, but that no Polish government could ever agree to Germany reannexing Danzig. Nor was he willing to join an outright alliance against Russia which would put Poland in a dangerous position. Beck, whose whole policy of despising and weakening the various schemes of collective security has often and rightly been criticized, has also, though less frequently, been attacked, at home and abroad, for reversing his older course and not giving in to Hitler at this stage. Nobody will ever know whether he would have acted differently if he could have clearly foreseen the price Poland was going to pay for her resistance. Nor is it possible to say what would have been Poland's fate if she had given in to Hitler and made herself an eastern annex to the Axis system. On the other hand Beck has with some justification been lauded for the courage with which he and his country faced, especially throughout the second quarter and the summer of 1939, the steadily increasing blackmail to which they were subjected. This courage has also sometimes been contrasted with the fact that Czechoslovakia, at Munich and in March 1939, capitulated without firing a shot. It is, however, very obvious that Czechoslovakia would never have capitulated if, instead of browbeating her into submission, the British and French governments had supported her resistance in the way in which they later, on March 31, 1939, acted in regard to Poland—by solemnly declaring that they would give this nation every support in their power if she were attacked by Hitler and resisted. Hitler himself would often claim that only this British guaranty had encouraged Poland to take what he considered an uncompromising stand in the face of an "extraordinarily generous German offer."

Be this as it may, at the moment Hitler's furious reaction in public found its nonpublic implementation in his directive to the armed forces, dated April 3, to prepare the war against Poland to begin on September 1. The very fact that this date was kept shows how definite Hitler's plans had become at this early stage.

Nevertheless it cannot yet be said that they had become irrevocable. There was still a great unknown quantity to be taken into account—the attitude of the Soviet Union—and Hitler could not possibly neglect it.

Moscow's policy of supporting plans for European collective security, represented and to an extent symbolized by Soviet Foreign Minister Litvinov, had during the last few years and months experienced a distinct setback. It had been much resented in Moscow that the four signatories at Munich saw nothing wrong in the fact that the Soviet Union, ally of both France and Czechoslovakia, had last October been left out in the cold. Only under the increasing pressure of public opinion did Britain's Conservative government finally decide for some cooperation with the Soviet Union in the attempt to contain Hitler's Germany. The general history of the failure of this half-hearted attempt, and of Moscow's eventual decision rather to go along with Hitler's suggestion for a close cooperation between Germany and Russia, goes far beyond the framework of this sketch. Yet one thing is clear: If in mid-August Stalin and his military advisers began to consider all further negotiations about a pact against Hitler as hopeless and senseless, at least one of the reasons for this was the attitude of Poland which, under the leadership of Foreign Minister Beck and Marshal Smigly-Rydż, refused permission for Russian troops to enter Polish territory even for the purpose of defending such territory in the case of a German attack. While historically as well as in the light of later events it may be quite understandable that Poland was reluctant to commit herself to this particular alliance, it is also quite clear that without it Poland was lost. The illusion that Poland, even in the case of more effective Franco-English support, but without any help from Russia, could withstand the full attack of the German air force and panzer armies was fantastic to begin with. The Polish decision was an awkward one in any case. As it turned out, it was a blind decision leading to total catastrophe.

The German campaign in Poland lasted less than a month and its outcome had been decided much sooner. At the time this was considered as a proof of the utter weakness of the Polish army. It was weak enough compared to its enemy's gigantic war machine, but it fought with the greatest bravery, and the fate, one year later, of the far larger, far better equipped and fully mobilized French army showed that Poland did not have to be ashamed of her sons.

Even before the end had come, Stalin sent his own army into Poland, in implementation of the secret clauses on the country's partitioning in the pact of friendship concluded on August 23 between the two dictators. There were, however, some changes: the clauses gave Lithuania to Stalin, and in Poland they gave Hitler most of the lands ethnically Polish, while Russia occupied mostly those regions whose inhabitants were predominantly Byelorussians and Ukrainians. Thus the Fifth Partition of Poland, in its results more pitiless and more horrifying by far than any of the preceding ones, left the great majority of the nation under one single rule, that of Nazi Germany.

It is difficult to exaggerate in speaking about the sadistic brutality of this occupation. Even there, however, subtle differences existed. The western parts of Poland, against all international law, were officially annexed by Germany. This did not only comprise territories which had once belonged to the Bismarckian Empire but also large parts of the former Russian Poland, including even Poland's second largest city, Łódź, which the Nazis renamed Litzmannstadt. This and the other annexed regions they proceeded to Germanize in the most pitiless way by transporting a large proportion of the Polish population into the eastern part of occupied Poland called the "Generalgouvernement," others as slave labor into Germany. This process of mass destruction was especially harsh and systematic in relation to the Polish intelligentsia whose members, as far as they had not succeeded in leaving the country, had often to go underground to escape the worst. At one stage the whole academic staff of the ancient Jagellon University in Cracow was put into concentration camps where many perished, and all institutions of higher learning were closed "for all times." Poles, if they deserved to live at all, could at best claim an existence as slaving robots.

No such claim, however, could be made by those three million Jews of Poland, the largest Jewish population in any European country. For them, and for millions of other European Jews, the Nazis built the gas chambers of Auschwitz (Oświecim), where alone hundreds of thousands were put to death, and many other less famous extermination camps. One of the most shocking and moving episodes in this well planned horror story was the fate of the Warsaw ghetto, where half a million Jews were slowly and systematically starved to death until, when this process became too slow, the Nazis sought other means and encountered the fierce and truly heroic resistance of the emaciated people behind the ghetto walls.

Slowly, in the course of those terrible war years, an army of Polish guerrilla fighters developed, which made things very uncomfortable for the Germans in a Poland which had, after June 1941, become the hinterland and basis for waging the war against the Soviet Union. The fate of much of this Polish underground army, fighting under the command of General Bór-Komorowski against the Nazis, was not a happy one. When, in August 1944, following repeated requests of Moscow radio for action, they rose in Warsaw, the Russian army—already within sight on the eastern shore of the Vistula—did not make use of this opportunity, and superior German troops annihilated the Poles before the Russian advance was resumed.

Yet, Polish soldiers, sailors, and airmen made remarkable contributions to the total war effort of the Allies outside Poland. Several divisions recruited from former prisoners of war in Russian hands were—since they were reluctant to fight with the Red Army—allowed to join Western armies via Persia. They fought in many places, especially in Africa and Italy. The small Polish navy, too, was repeatedly and creditably in action.

The Czechoslovak contribution to the allied war effort was also far from insignificant. Ground troops of some strength achieved successes already in April 1943, in the Kharkov region, and reinforced the Russian onslaught against the Nazis and their satellites in the Carpathian sector during the winter 1944-45. Czechoslovak airmen took a notable part in the work of the Coastal Command of Britain's Royal Air Force, and thereby, although fighters from a landlocked country, they helped in the winning of the Battle of the Atlantic.

It is one of the tragic facts of the later phase of the war and the immediate postwar period that the participation of the West Slav nations in the war on the Western front and under Western high commands was, in the states that came to exist within the Soviet orbit, not only left unrecognized but was even considered as a sort of incriminating fact. Perhaps it was to some extent understandable that in Russia the activities of the Polish underground army was looked upon with distrust since there was little doubt about the strongly anti-Russian feelings of large groups among those Polish fighters, feelings increasingly shared, especially after the unfortunate accidental death of General Sikorski, the head of the Polish émigré government, by many of the "London Poles." But no such attitude could be suspected by the Russians in regard to Czechs and Slovaks, the great majority of whom were friendly to Russia. Yet after the war, or at least after 1948, only the Czechoslovak troops trained in Russia and active on the Eastern front, and the partisans who fought in the anti-Tiso and anti-German uprising in Slovakia in 1944, were glorified as true patriots. (Only very recently have at least the outstanding feats of Czechoslovak airmen in the West occasionally been remembered in Czechoslovak publications with the respect they deserve.)

If we look back today upon the fate of the West Slav nations under the brutal yoke of Naziism, the outstanding fact is their very survival as nations, to an extent that during the postwar era, despite the additional burdens of the Cold War and of Stalinist pressure put upon them, they were still able to make remarkable efforts and achieve impressive successes in revival and reconstruction. And in this regard the Polish achievement is clearly the most outstanding. No other nation had been so thoroughly ground under the feet of the conquerors, no other had lost such a large proportion of her leading citizens in almost any field of endeavor. Yet a Poland worthy of the name and conscious of her great traditions exists again.

The Czech territories, on the other hand, were better off because there was—except for the very last stages of the war—no fighting going on, and because the losses owing to Nazi actions, especially by mass executions and by economic ruin, was counted "only" in thousands, not, as in Poland, in tens or hundreds of thousands. In the "Protectorate" too, however, the ultimate German intention was to do away with the existence of a strong Slavic nation in what was considered German "Lebensraum," partly by assimilation—if the Czechs were ready to be assimilated—partly by resettlement, and if necessary by wholesale extermination. The main reason why this scheme was not furthered more effectively during the six years of Nazi occupation was the fact that the German war machine was thought to need, for the duration, not only the great industrial apparatus which had so cheaply been gained in 1939, but also most of the people who had to serve it. All the greater was the German fury over the many successful sabotage acts. The grim policy of "Butcher" Reinhard Heydrich led to his assassination in May 1942, and this again to mass execution and to the total destruction of the town of Lidice, where all males were killed, all women and children deported. (It was only the first such act, followed by many similar acts all over Eastern Europe and even in France.) But it did not destroy the Czech will and capacity for effective resistance.

Slovakia, officially supposed to be Germany's ally rather than her victim, fared better, especially during the early years of the war when the German policy wanted to prove how happy even a small Slavic nation could be in Hitler's new order. But deep dissatisfaction with the Nazi exploitation and with the Tuka regime, which more and more identified itself with the Nazi state, led eventually to one of the strongest partisan rebellions of the war, started in August 1944 and led by the underground Slovak National Council. While eventually the Communists claimed most of the credit for organizing it they were, in fact, only a minority among the partisans, whose numbers rose as many of the Slovak army units sent against them by the Bratislava government went over to them. Unfortunately, the help of the approaching Red Army, which the leaders of the movement had counted on, was not forthcoming to the extent that would have prevented effective German counteraction. Even so, the sacrifice was not in vain: a number of German divisions, badly needed elsewhere, were tied down, and the threat of the partisans in the Slovak mountains did not cease until, around the turn of the year, the Red Army, with Czech and Slovak units, marched in. On the whole, the population of all of Czechoslovakia, unlike the Polish people, regarded the Red Army as liberators. A special story, however, was the liberation of Prague. The city, in the beginning of June 1945, rose against the Germans just as Paris had risen in 1944. The Germans tried hard but in vain to suppress the rising, but there were difficult moments when it looked as if the German army might still, as it had in Warsaw, succeed in destroying the rebellion. The nearest Allied army, at this moment, was Patton's Third Army in the Pilsen region, but they did not move because the Russian High Command had demanded that the right to liberate Prague should belong to the Red Army alone, and this urgent request was considered to be binding. In the outcome this fact had considerable influence upon further developments in Czechoslovakia, especially since the Czech Communists, for a long time, claimed that the failure of the Americans to assist the Czech rising in Prague showed their lack of interest in Czech freedom (or even worse motives than that). The feeling that Czechoslovakia, in moments of crisis, could never count on the West—a feeling going back to the days of Munich—thus was strengthened again and helps to explain much that happened after 1945.

This development, in both countries, has already been discussed in Chapter One. There remains perhaps one aspect of their history that should be referred to in conclusion. The relation between the West Slav states and their peoples has fluctuated between harmony and conflict, and it is hardly a mistake to say that conflicts between them were more frequent than phases of neighborly harmony, and that, especially after the end of World War I, little love was lost between them. Frequent and even traditional conflict between brothers, between near ethnic relatives, is nothing new in history, but in few cases in history has it had such fatal consequences as in this one. Perhaps one can hope, in the case of Poland and Czechoslovakia, that this sad and unprofitable tradition has now been broken. If this should prove to be true, it would be partly because of their bitter experiences during the period leading to World War II, partly also because of the common impact of Communist ideology and Moscow politics. The latter, however, should not be overrated. To some extent a better understanding between the West Slav nations and especially the intelligentsia of both countries has even emerged from the common need to maintain a measure of independence in relation to the overwhelming strength of the great Slavic brother. This independence will remain limited, especially as long as the Cold War has not been liquidated and as long as there is—as at present—a real and deep worry in Eastern Europe concerning the possible activization of what is considered to be German revisionism and revanchism. For this reason Warsaw and Prague, the latter with even less inhibitions than the former, will look upon Russia as the only true guaranty for continued political existence. In the long run this fear may be reduced or eliminated.

But the closer the two West Slav states can come to one another, the better are also the chances for their occupying a position of some permanent importance in international affairs which would have to be respected by East and West alike.

SUGGESTED READINGS

The historiography on and by the nations of Poland and Czechoslovakia is vast and has a long and honorable tradition. In its medieval beginnings it usually took, as that of most other European nations belonging to the Roman Catholic world, the form of chronicles written in Latin. Among them the first outstanding achievement was the *Chronicon Bohemorum,* written by the Prague canon Cosmas during the first quarter of the twelfth century. The first important Polish chronicler was Vincent Kadłubek, bishop of Cracow (d. 1223). In the later thirteenth century there appeared in Bohemia the first chronicler to use the Czech language in the rhymed chronicle of the so-called Dalimil. But the first West Slav chronicler who probably deserves to be considered as a true historian of high qualities was Jan Długosz, a member of the Polish high clergy and an important servant of King Casimir IV whose huge work is still a rich source not only for the history of Poland but also of other parts of Central and Eastern Europe, including fifteenth-century Bohemia and Hungary (*Opera omnia,* ed. A. Przezdziecki, Vols. 5-9, Cracow: 1873-78).

A truly critical modern historiography had, of course, to wait for the nineteenth century. We have, in the text, met with two historians who, each in his own way, were leaders of their nations—Lelewel and Palacký. The latter's main work especially (*Geschichte von Böhmen,* 5 vols. in 11, 1864 and later), while now in many ways outdated, is still useful, as it can be read in German as well as Czech. Its German edition has never been fully superseded by the much shorter *Geschichte Böhmens* by A. Bachmann (2 vols., Gotha: 1899-1905). Both works go only to 1526, the date of the Hapsburgs' succession to the throne of Bohemia, but Palacký's work is far more detailed and has had enormous influence upon the later development of Czech historiography. A similarly detailed presentation by a German historian of an especially important period of Polish history, dating from the same time, is Jacob Caro's *Geschichte Polens* (Gotha: 1863-88).

Proceeding to modern works we shall list mainly, though not exclusively, writings in English. For the general background, see Francis Dvorník's *The Slavs, Their Early History and Civilizations* (Boston: 1956), and his *The Slavs in European History and Civilization* (New Brunswick: 1962), the latter work being especially valuable for the breadth of its approach and its extraordinarily comprehensive bibliographical notes. It only goes as far as the eighteenth century. Another valuable background volume is Oscar Halecki's *Borderlands of Western Civilization, A History of East Central Europe*, which goes down to modern times. It concentrates, more than does Dvorník, upon political history. From the same author we also have a well organized short, one-volume *History of Poland* (rev. ed., London and New York: 1955/1956). The same topic—the whole course of Polish history from its early beginnings to the end of the Piłsudski era—is treated in more detail in *The Cambridge History of Poland*, edited by Reddaway, Penson, Halecki, and Dyboski. Of its two volumes the second (from 1697, that is, the beginning of the "Saxon Period") appeared in 1941, when Poland was still under German occupation and some of the work's Polish contributors were either in concentration camps or had perished. The first volume was, partly for these reasons, published only in 1950. While uneven, the work is nevertheless of the greatest value for the presentation of Polish history to the English-speaking world, especially if used in combination, for cultural issues, with Roman Dyboski's *Poland in World Civilization* (New York: 1950). No work of comparable comprehensiveness exists, as yet, in English on the total history of Czechoslovakia. The best one-volume account is S. H. Thomson's *Czechoslovakia in European History* (2nd ed., Princeton: 1953), with an especially fine chapter on the Czech Reformation. A somewhat earlier work finished during the war, *A History of the Czechs and Slovaks* (London: 1943), by R. W. Seton-Watson, complements Thomson's work by a detailed treatment of the Czech and Slovak developments inside the nineteenth- and early twentieth-century Hapsburg Empire (a new edition in 1965).

As for the treatment of special periods in English there is the translation of a work on Polish beginnings, Zygmunt Wojciechoswki's *Mieszko I and the Rise of the Polish State* (Toruń: 1936), and Dvorník's *The Making of Central and Eastern Europe* (London: 1949). For most of the important fourteenth century, Western readers are still dependent on non-English works such as those by Palacký and Caro, as well as E. Werunsky's *Geschichte Kaiser Karls IV und seiner Zeit* (4 vols., Innsbruck: 1880-92). There is, however, a somewhat romantic monograph in English on the last years of the fourteenth century by Charlotte H. Kellog, *Jadwiga, Poland's Great Queen* (New York: 1931).

There is a good deal more in English on the two nations in the fifteenth century. The Hussite movement, especially, has found considerable interest in the West. The figure of Hus himself was the subject of a pioneering monograph by Count Lützow, *The Life and Times of Master John Huss* (London: 1909). Another still valuable treatment of the development and the religious significance of Hus and his adherents is contained in Bishop Mandel Creighton's *History of the Papacy from the Great Schism to the Sack of Rome* (Vol. II, London: 1899). See further Matthew Spinka's short but instructive *John Hus and the Czech Reform* (Chicago: 1941) and his more profoundly conceived *John Hus' Concept of the Church* (Princeton: 1966). Of interest is also Ernest Denis' work *Hus et la guerre des Hussites* (Paris: 1878). On the Hussite Revolution after Hus see F. G. Heymann, *John Žižka and the Hussite Revolution* (Princeton: 1955). For the present Czech-Marxian interpretation of this movement see J. Macek, *The Hussite Movement in Bohemia* (2nd ed., Prague: 1958). See further the articles by H. Kaminsky, "Hussite Radicalism and the Origin of Tábor," *Medievalia et Humanistica* (Boulder: 1956), and his "Chiliasm and the Hussite Revolution," *Church History*, 1957. For the Poděbradian period see F. G. Heymann, *George of Bohemia, King of Heretics* (Princeton: 1965), and concentrating especially on the conflict with the papacy, Otakar Odložilík's *The Hussite King*, New Brunswick 1965. Of the growing literature on the movement of the Czech Brethren, born during the Poděbradian age and fully developed under the Jagellons in Bohemia and Moravia, there is an excellent monograph by Peter Brock, *The Political and Social Doctrines of the Unity of Czech Brethren in the Fifteenth and Early Sixteenth Centuries* (The Hague: 1957). For the period from George of Poděbrady to 1620 see also E. Denis, *La fin de l'indépendence bohême* (Paris: 1878).

With the appearance of the German-Swiss Reformation there is again more material in English on the Polish scene. See, for a partial exploration, Paul Fox, *The Reformation in Poland, Some Social and Economic Aspects* (Baltimore: 1924). The history of the Polish anti-Trinitarians is presented with much interest by E. M. Wilbur in his *History of Unitarianism* (2 vols., Cambridge, Mass.: 1945-52), and in George H. Williams, *The Radical Reformation* (Philadelphia: 1962), but the chief authority in the field is the Cracow-based Polish church historian Stanisław Kot. Among his many studies presented in several languages the most important in English is his *Socinianism in Poland* (Boston: 1957). The Catholic development during the pre-Reformation and Reformation period in Poland, in the context of European developments, is treated by O. Halecki in *From Florence to Brest, 1439-1596* (New York: 1959).

There is rather little in English on either of the two countries in the period of the Thirty Years' War and the later seventeenth century. The story of the Czech emigration and its background is told by Ernest Sommer, *Into Exile, The History of the Counter-Reformation in Bohemia, 1620-1650* (London: 1943). For some of Wallenstein's problems and Bohemian background consult the German edition of J. Pekař's *Wallenstein, 1630-1634* (Berlin: 1937). There are, however, monographs on some great figures of the time, in the Czech orbit particularly on Comenius—two of them, both highly instructive, written by American scholars of Czech background for his 350th birthday anniversary, O. Odložilík, *Jan Amos Komenský*, and M. Spinka, *John Amos Comenius, that Incomparable Moravian*, both published in Chicago, 1942 and 1943. More specialized is F. F. Young's study *Comenius in England* (Oxford: 1932).

The background of late seventeenth-century Poland is illuminated by two English publications on Jan Sobieski, both called *Sobieski, King of Poland*, one by John B. Morton (London: 1932), the other a translation from the Polish of Otton Laskowski (Glasgow: 1944). Readers of German may profit even more by turning to the colorful account of Otto Forst-Battaglia, *Jan Sobieski, König von Polen* (Zürich: 1946), matched in liveliness by the same author's *Stanisław August Poniatowski und der Ausgang des alten Polenstaates* (Berlin: 1927). Important for the understanding of the later history of the "Royal Republic" is also Władysław Konopczyński's comparative study, *Le liberum veto* (Paris: 1930).

For the late eighteenth century, there is next to nothing in English, and not much in other Western languages, on the Saxon period, and in Bohemian history there is just one valuable monograph by R. J. Kerner, *Bohemia in the Eighteenth Century* (New York: 1932), mostly dealing with the short reign of Emperor Leopold II. There is also a valuable French contribution to Czech developments in the later seventeenth and eighteenth centuries, E. Denis' *La Bohême depuis la Montagne Blanche* (2 vols., Paris: 1930).

American historians have paid considerable attention to the various partitions of Poland. See above all the recent excellent study by Herbert H. Kaplan, *The First Partition of Poland* (New York: 1962). An older work but still distinguished as a fine treatment mainly of the aspects of diplomatic history is Robert H. Lord's *The Second Partition of Po-*

land (Cambridge, Mass.: 1915). For the intervening period of moral and intellectual recovery see W. G. Rose's work *Stanisław Konarski* (London: 1929). Developments of the Third Partition and the resistance against Russia and Prussia are at least partly covered by the devoted English Polonophile Monica M. Gardner's *Kościuszko, a Biography* (2nd ed., London: 1942).

In relation to the nineteenth century, when Poland's intellectual life and her hopes for national rebirth were so strongly tied to France and the Polish emigration in that country, it was perhaps natural that publications in French, though mainly written by Poles and translated, prevail over those in English. There is a valuable work by the Polish historian Szymon Askenazi, *Napoléon et la Pologne* (Paris: 1903). Two works by Poles on developments connected with the emigration in France are Marceli Handelsman's *Les idées françaises et la mentalité politique de la Pologne au XIXe siècle* (Paris: 1927), and Michal Sokolnicki's *Les origines de l'émigration polonaise en France* (Paris: 1931). An important contribution in German translation by a Pole (despite the name) is Wilhelm Feldman's *Geschichte der politischen Ideen in Polen seit dessen Teilungen* (Leipzig: 1917), dealing mostly with the five decades preceding World War I. Poland's greatest political figure in the period from the partitions to the second revolution against Russia and the background of his work are impressively presented by the Polish general and historian Marian Kukiel in his *Czartoryski and European Unity 1770-1861* (Princeton: 1955), while the first revolution and the developments leading up to it are depicted by R. F. Leslie, *Polish Politics and the Revolution of November 1830* (London and New York: 1956.)

For the history, after 1848, of the West Slavs (and other ethnic groups) under Hapsburg rule the indispensable standard work is Robert Kann's *The Multinational Empire: Nationalism and National Reform in the Habsburg Monarchy 1848-1918* (2 vols., New York: 1950). The fate of the Poles in Germany in the last decades before World War I is treated by Richard W. Sims, *Germanizing Prussian Poland* (New York: 1941).

On the development leading through World War I to independence there are important testimonies by some of the main actors. A preparatory work, explaining the author's own political ideas, was Roman Dmowski's *La question polonaise* (Paris: 1909). His great antagonist Piłsudski's reminiscences are available in a shortened English translation, *Memories of a Polish Revolutionary Soldier* (London: 1931), and his account of his actions in the Russo-Polish War in the French publication *L'année 1920* (Paris: 1929.) For developments in Poland itself during the war see the detailed treatment in the collective work by M. Handelsman and others, *La Pologne, sa vie économique et sociale pendant la guerre* (2 vols., Paris: 1933, 1939). For the diplomatic prehistory and history of the restitution of Polish and Czechoslovak independence see, as an excellent introduction, looked at from this side of the Atlantic, Victor S. Mamatey, *The United States and East Central Europe: A Study of Wilsonian Diplomacy and Propaganda* (Princeton: 1957). The policy of the other side is treated by E. R. Burke, *The Polish Policy of the Central Powers during the World War* (Chicago: 1936). The complete diplomatic history of the liberation of each of the two countries is told in Titus Komarnicki's *Rebirth of the Polish Republic, 1914-1920* (London: 1957), and D. Perman's *The Shaping of the Czechoslovak State, 1914-1920* (Leiden: 1962); the latter contains a very objective report on the fateful Teschen dispute. Among the chief leaders and negotiators, the Czechs have been more intent to report their activities and political views; for example, Masaryk in *The New Europe* (New York: 1918) and *The Making of a State* (London: 1927), and Beneš in *My War Memoirs* (Boston: 1928). Among the considerable number of biographies of both men perhaps Donald A. Lowrie's *Masaryk of Czechoslovakia* (London: 1937), Edward P. Newman's *Masaryk* (London: 1961), and Odložilík's short but enlightening *Masaryk's Idea of Democracy* (New York: 1952), should be named. Very valuable are also Karel Čapek's dialogues with Masaryk, published in English under the title *President Masaryk Tells his Story* (London: 1934). Beneš's figure is, even now, much more controversial. Among a number of biographies, most of them based on his role prior to World War II, the best is perhaps E. B. Hitchcock's *Beneš, The Man and the Statesman* (London: 1940). His diplomacy has been well and fairly analyzed by Paul E. Zinner in G. Craig and F. Gilbert ed., *The Diplomats, 1919-1939* (pp. 100-22). No comparable wealth exists in English on the founders and leading statesmen of Poland. On Paderewski there is an English biography, Ch. Philipp's *Paderewski* (New York: 1934). A good book on Piłsudski in English is W. F. Reddaway's *Marshal Piłsudski* (London: 1939).

For the period between the wars there is no completely adequate specialized treatment in English on either country. Hugh Seton-Watson's *Eastern Europe between the Wars* (Cambridge: 1945) is still valuable. Some additional aspects can be found in the more recent *Independent Eastern Europe*, by C. A. Macartney and A. W. Palmer (London: 1962). Robert Machrey's *The Poland of Piłsudski* (New York: 1937), is good as far as it goes—that is 1936, about the same date at which the *Cambridge History of Poland* ends. Far more detailed and complete is the French account in the collective work edited by J. Modzelewski, *Pologne 1919-1939* (3 vols., Neuchatel: 1945-47). The same period in Czechoslovakia is presented by R. J. Kerner, ed., *Czechoslovakia: Twenty Years of Independence* (Berkeley: 1940). Special issues are covered by Josef Chmelař, *Political Parties in Czechoslovakia* (Prague: 1926); Lucy Textor, *Land Reform in Czechoslovakia* (London: 1923); Bracket Lewis, *Facts about Democracy in Czechoslovakia.* An early and very fair discussion of the Sudeten German problem is that by the Czech philosopher Emanuel Radl, *Der Kampf zwischen Deutschen und Tschechen* (Reichenberg: 1928). More sharply focused on the political troubles is the work by Elizabeth Wiskemann, *Czechs and Germans* (London: 1938). For the specific problems of Slovakia during the Masaryk republic one of the most valuable contributions is a collective work of leading Slovaks edited by R. W. Seton-Watson, *Slovakia Then and Now, A Political Survey* (London: 1931). There is, however, no really good comprehensive history of Slovakia in any language, and the recent publication of such histories in the United States suffer from the fact that their authors—who had played some role on one side or the other during the break-up of Czechoslovakia in 1939 and during the Tiso Republic—now feel the need of defending their policy. Thus, for uninhibited Slovak separatism, see the works of J. M. Kirschbaum, *Slovakia* (New York: 1960) and J. A. Mikus, *Slovakia, a Political History 1918-1950* (Milwaukee: 1963), and, on the other side, J. Lettrich, *History of Modern Slovakia* (New York: 1953). A substantial and essentially objective history of the Slovaks still remains to be written. The nearest approach to it appears, somewhat ironically, to be a very thorough, erudite, and unprejudiced work written by a Hungarian scholar, and published, so far only in parts, in Germany: Ludwig von Gogolák, *Beiträge zur Geschichte des slowakischen Volkes* (Vol. I, 1526-1790, Munich: 1963).

There is a large and still growing literature in English and other languages on the catastrophic developments of the years 1938 and 1939, much of it contained in the memoirs and publications of statesmen and diplomats, themselves engaged in the events. The best English-written work on Munich is J. W. Wheeler-Bennett's *Munich: Prologue to Tragedy* (New York: 1948), but what appears to be a well-nigh definitive account is the work of a Czech in German, Boris Čelovský, *Das Münchner Abkommen von 1938* (Stuttgart: 1958). The immediate follow-up in regard to Poland is described by France's ambassador to Warsaw Leon Noel, *L'aggression allemande contre la Pologne* (Paris: 1946). Foreign Minister Beck's unfortunate policy is defended by himself in *Dernier rapport: Politique polonaise 1926-1939* (Neuchatel: 1951), as well as by his assistant Jan Szembek, *Journal, 1933-1939* (Paris: 1952). See also Stanisław Mackiewicz, *Colonel Beck and his Policy* (London: 1944). The earlier quoted collective work *The Diplomats* (Princeton: 1953) also contains a valuable chapter on Beck by Henry L. Roberts (pp. 579-614). The story of war and occupation has again been told in many forms and from many quarters. Polish military leaders have reported on their exploits: General W. Anders, commander of the Second Polish Corps, in *An Army in Exile* (New York: 1949), and General Bór-Komorowski, leader of Poland's underground forces, in *The Secret Army* (New York: 1951). See also S. Korbonski, *Fighting Warsaw, the Story of the Polish Underground State* (New York: 1956). On the immediate sequel in Poland, apart from the many treatments of the beginning of the Cold War, see Stanisław Mikolajczyk, *The Rape of Poland* (New York: 1948). On Czechoslovakia during the time of the occupation see Sheila Grant Duff, *A German Protectorate: The Czechs under Nazi Rule* (New York: 1942). Beneš's second war memoirs, *From Munich to New War and New Victory* (Boston: 1957), is less of a monument to its author than the earlier volume. The events leading up to the Communist take-over in Prague are presented by Josef Korbel in *The Communist Subversion of Czechoslovakia* (Princeton: 1959). The following 12 years are treated in a thorough and not overpolemical way by Edward Táborský, *Communism in Czechoslovakia 1948-1960* (Princeton: 1961). There is no corresponding work on Poland. Richard Staar's *Poland 1944-1962, The Sovietization of a Captive People* is too grimly hostile to be acceptable as a judicious exploration of the field, though it contains valuable statistical material. The causes, the development and the consequences of the unbloody near-revolution of 1956 is told extremely well by a brilliant newspaper woman, Flora Lewis, *A Case History of Hope* (New York: 1958).

There is a vast treasure of works written in the West Slav languages to which anyone interested in a detailed study of the history of those nations has to turn. The standard works include two significant collective works on Polish history, one, by W. Antoniewicz and others, reaching to 1914: *Polska, jej dzieje i kultura od czasów najdawniejszych do chwili obecnej* (*Poland, its history and culture from the oldest times to the present*) (3 vols., Warsaw: 1928-32); and the new *Historia Polski* (*History of Poland*) (Warsaw: 1957 and after), directed by T. Manteuffel and written by a number of prominent historians of the present, thus showing also the changed interpretations which, to some extent, were imposed by the policies of the post-World War II Poland. The work is organized in three main parts, each divided into several volumes.

An even more ambitious venture was started in Prague in 1912 by the prominent Czech historian Václav Novotný. It was called *České dějiny* (*Bohemian history*) and was published by the great scientific publishing house of Jan Laichter, in the expectation of presenting the whole history of the Czech nation from its earliest beginnings to the twentieth century. The work goes on and is still far from finished. At present it reaches from the beginning to 1464, with two missing volumes out of 16 and with an average length of 800 pages per volume. The huge enterprise, now under the direction of the Historical Institute of the Czechoslovak Academy of Sciences, will continue, with the few lacunae and the Jagiellon phase to be written in the near future. It is, and hopefully will remain, a work of which Czechoslovak historiography can be proud.

To these publications also belong two works, one Polish and one Czech, concerned with the mutual historical impact of the two nations. Both are collective enterprises. The Polish work, written by T. Lehr-Splawiński and two others, is called *Polska-Czechy, Dziesięć wieków sasiedztwa* (*Poland-Bohemia, Neighbors through ten centuries*). The Czech work, edited by J. Macůrek and written by a dozen scholars, is called *Češi a Poláci v minulosti* (*Czechs and Poles in past history*). Of two planned volumes, only the first, reaching to the early eighteenth century, is published so far (Prague: 1964). Both publications hoped to contribute to the better understanding between Poland and Czechoslovakia.

Finally, there is a recent production called *The Czechoslovak Contribution to World Culture*, edited by Miloslav Rechcígl, published under the auspices of the Czechoslovak Society of Arts and Sciences in America by Mouton (the Hague: 1964). Of the 53 contributors, specialists in many different fields, the great majority (44) are people born in Czechoslovakia. The book, while naturally uneven in the value of so many contributions, shows to the reader, in a way comparable to Dyboski's *Poland in World Civilization*, the rich contributions that have been made by Czech and Slovak people in every single cultural field of importance. Not the least merit of the work is a "Selective Bibliography in the Western European Languages."

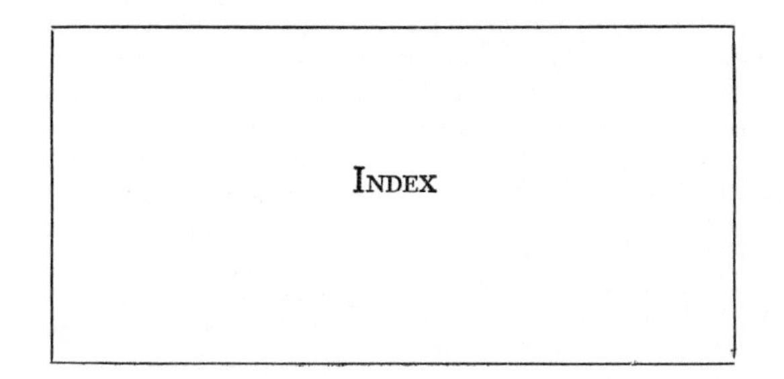

INDEX

The Modern Nations in Historical Perspective Series

The American Assembly Series

AUTOMATION AND TECHNOLOGICAL CHANGE,
edited by John T. Dunlop—S-AA-7

THE CONGRESS AND AMERICA'S FUTURE,
edited by David B. Truman—S-AA-13

THE COURTS, THE PUBLIC, AND THE LAW EXPLOSION,
edited by Harry W. Jones—S-AA-15

THE FEDERAL GOVERNMENT SERVICE (Second Edition),
edited by Wallace S. Sayre—S-AA-14

GOALS FOR AMERICANS: The Report of the President's
Commission on National Goals—S-AA-3

OUTER SPACE: Prospects for Man and Society,
edited by Lincoln P. Bloomfield—S-AA-5

THE POPULATION DILEMMA,
edited by Philip M. Hauser—S-AA-10

THE SECRETARY OF STATE,
edited by Don K. Price—S-AA-2

THE UNITED STATES AND CANADA,
edited by John Sloan Dickey—S-AA-12

THE UNITED STATES AND THE FAR EAST (Second Edition),
edited by Willard L. Thorp—S-AA-6

THE UNITED STATES AND JAPAN,
edited by Herbert Passin—S-AA-16

THE UNITED STATES AND LATIN AMERICA (Second Edition),
edited by Herbert L. Matthews—S-AA-9

THE UNITED STATES AND THE MIDDLE EAST,
edited by Georgiana G. Stevens—S-AA-11

The Eyewitness Accounts of American History Series

The American Labor Movement,
edited by Leon Litwack—S-44
American Socialism, 1900-1960,
edited by H. Wayne Morgan—S-85
The Causes of the Civil War,
edited by Kenneth M. Stampp (with revisions)—S-1
The Great Depression,
edited by David A. Shannon—S-10
Immigration as a Factor in American History,
edited by Oscar Handlin—S-2
The Negro Since Emancipation,
edited by Harvey Wish—S-106
The New Deal and the American People,
edited by Frank Freidel—S-87
The Progressive Movement: 1900-1915,
edited by Richard Hofstadter—S-72
Reconstruction, 1865-1877,
edited by Richard N. Current—S-114
Slavery Attacked: The Abolitionist Crusade,
edited by John L. Thomas—S-109
Slavery Defended: The Views of the Old South,
edited by Eric L. McKitrick—S-59
The Twenties: Fords, Flappers and Fanatics,
edited by George E. Mowry—S-69